Political History

POLITICAL HISTORY

PRINCIPLES AND PRACTICE

BY G. R. ELTON

BASIC BOOKS, INC., PUBLISHERS

NEW YORK : LONDON

© 1970 by Basic Books, Inc.
Library of Congress Catalog Card Number: 75–110768
SBN 465–05894–9
Manufactured in the United States of America
DESIGNED BY VINCENT TORRE

PREFACE

The invitation to reflect on the methods, purposes, and possibilities of political history has given me a welcome opportunity to develop a little further some of the points I briefly sketched in my *Practice of History*, as well as to consider some additional matters arising out of the actual work of studying and writing history. I could perhaps wish that I had been more systematic, but the indulgent critic may appreciate that this relative lack of order itself reflects realities about historical writing which a more precise and philosophical approach obscures. I know that I may seem to have repeated myself too often but would argue that one of the striking things about these enquiries is the manner in which the same issues arise as different lines of approach are tried: the contents of this kind of history and the problems of its necessary methods are seen to be remarkably interrelated. That very probably I have not succeeded in taking any part of the argument to a final conclusion I should be very far from denying: but that, too, is in the nature of history.

G.R.E.

Clare College, Cambridge
September 1969

CONTENTS

Political History

CHAPTER 1

The Categories

1. A Definition

War and peace, plots and revolutions, the births and marriages and deaths of kings. Statesmen and ambassadors, bureaucrats and union leaders, priests and peasants. The recorded lives of people, of nations, of mankind.

Political history is the history of politics, and politics are the activities of men in society. Not all life is activity, and politics are not at all the whole of life, even in society. As everybody knows, Aristotle called man a "political animal," but what he meant by *zoon politikon* was a social animal, an animal congregated in a *polis*—an animal given to living in company with its kind and forming organized groups to do so. What we understand by the political side of man's nature, on the other hand, refers essentially to the active expression of this social organism, its dynamic manifestation. Insofar as men are social, they *are;* as political beings they *do.*

Therefore, political history is the study of that dynamic activity in the past experience of human societies which has direct relevance to the organizational aspects of those societies. That is to say, it is concerned with those activities which arise from the fact that men create, maintain, transform, and destroy social structures in which they live. Dynamic activity depends on the presence of a force—on the employment of energy—and the force applicable to political action is power: the power to do things for, or to, other people. Power constitutes the essential theme of political history. This type of history describes the way in which men strive for power and use it inside their own societies: it tells of personal battles for ascendancy, the maintenance and exercise of rule, the achievement of power through organization (political parties, elections) and all the details which appear, as it were, on the front page of the historical newspaper. Second, it describes the active exercise of power between societies, the international politics of conventional speech, as distinct from those that are internal to this or that state. The subject matter of political history is, therefore, that agglomerate of "affairs" which at one time constituted in effect the whole content of written history. Nowadays, the questions we ask of the past have proliferated; we want to know not only what men did in public life, but how they lived (social history), how they organized wealth (economic history), what and how they thought (intellectual history), how they expressed their sense of beauty (history of art), and so on.

A good many people think of political history as a very old-fashioned way of looking at the past, even as a boring form of study and as not very civilized. There is nothing at all to be said for such attitudes: historians who can muster no interest for the active political lives of past societies have no sense of history at all. The first historical writing was, rightly, political. When Herodotus described the wars between Greeks and barbarians, or Thucydides those between Greek and Greek, they were moved by the desire to perpetuate the memory of great events, and they knew well enough that the events were great because massive struggles for power—for liberty or dominance, ascendancy or accom-

modation, tolerance or constraint—had taken place. Like
all the classic historians of mankind, they sought the elevated theme and found it in politics. There have even been
men like Gibbon, determined to be historians without any
idea what history they might wish to write, until some accident revealed the great subject to them. And always the
subject has formed itself around the acquisition and use of
power, around its abuse and loss. Men's collective tragedies
and comedies are political; the tragic and comical history of
mankind needs primarily to attend to politics and power.

Moreover, whatever else history may be, it must at heart
be a story, a story of the changing fortunes of men, and
political history therefore comes first because, above all the
forms of historical study, it wants to, even needs to, tell a
story. The activities concerned with power take place in
chronological sequence and display themselves as a tale,
though admittedly an extremely complicated one which cannot always flow steadily onward. Unlike more descriptive
and analytical historians, the political historian is profoundly concerned to know what *happened*—exactly what
happened. He wishes to follow the fortunes of a man, a
party, an army, or a country through time, and when he has
related how things happened, he has done his job. This
sounds simple, but the how, properly told, includes a great
deal more than a mere delineation of events, one after
another. It includes, for instance, the problem of why men
did things, or attempted or failed to do them; their thoughts,
ambitions, and mistakes are part of the story. Neither the
people nor the events of political history are uncomplicated
particles, readily identified and set down to make a story. I
hope to show, in due course, how complicated the political
narrative really can and should be. Nevertheless, awareness
of complexity must not make the political historian forget
his first purpose: to relate the tale of action and reaction.
He must extract his account of action from the confusion

of past lives and concentrate on following the development step by step. At its purest, political history gets as self-contained and remote from the realities of the historical experience as do the other forms of historical writing when, tackling their proper theme, they forget, for instance, the existence of politics. Pure political history of this kind, at one time very common because no one had worked out the alternative ways of writing history, still occasionally gets written even today; and when some theme cannot readily be unraveled any other way, the method, in principle unsatisfactory, remains justified.

This method, usually encountered when a set of hitherto unexplored political papers first attracts the historian, may be illustrated by an example which shows the virtues and deficiencies of the genre. In the history of England, the years 1915–1925 were filled with all sorts of things: war, peace, economic depression, social upheaval, a revolution in manners. They include also the phenomenon known as the decline of the Liberal party. Wishing to discuss this, Trevor Wilson decided that an adequate account and explanation could be given by following the day-to-day doings and purposes of a group of politicians who are shown pursuing their immediate ends—narrowly political ends in the struggle of personalities and parties—as though no other activity existed for them and around them.[1]* However one judges the actual operation—and in its own terms the book is a very good one—this concentrated abstraction of one particular theme manifestly distorts the complex reality even of the political struggles of those years. Even in political terms, the decline of a party with a national organization and appeal cannot be described by looking at its central organization and figures only; and the sudden withdrawal of electoral support surely requires some investigation of social groups, supporting interests, and the movement of opinion. Never-

* Notes for this chapter begin on p. 54.

theless, Wilson not only wrote an interesting and relevant book, but justified his adoption of a method which excludes so much else of relevance. The rivalries of politicians were indeed an essential precondition of their party's collapse. Thus Wilson for the first time makes clear *how* the party declined, and in the course of this telling of *how* a good deal of the *why* also emerges. And until a story has achieved the sort of clarity here displayed, arguments about the various other circumstances which can be seen or conjectured to have played their part remain highly speculative. Thus even the purely political narrative continues its justified existence where its main task, the unraveling of the story, has not yet been performed. Not only does the world of political activity—the world of power—deserve to have its story told, but unless the story is told no other attendant history can be usefully investigated.

However, a great many stories have been told, so that for much history this restricted kind of political history is no longer suitable. This does not mean that political history must be confined to the unexplored, for I hope to show how much more comprehensive and thickly textured the treatment can be while yet remaining strictly political history. But while political history may and must enlarge its compass and interests, it must also retain its characteristic shape and purpose. That the political story in fact takes place in a welter of circumstances not themselves political is perfectly true: the social structure of the political society, the personal lives of its members, the economic concerns of the people, the philosophies and religions and sciences which are active in their own right but also influence political action by creating influential ways of thinking, all these contribute something to the needs of the political historian. The history of politics, like all other sectional history, unrolls in front of an amalgam made up of strictly nonpolitical (nonactive and not power-determined) elements in man's historical experience. It is not the function of political history to investigate or describe these other things, even though the political historian well may be, and usually must be, thoroughly aware of them and understand their relation to his politics. His chosen task remains the telling of a story concerned with the analysis of power and its uses in human social relationships. The expansion beyond the straight or old-fashioned type of story which he must seek has nothing to do with the nonpolitical lives of men, but with those political realities (often seemingly embedded in nonpolitical areas) that are not immediately apparent as political. To take a very simple example: it is possible to describe the battle over some piece of legislation in terms of the debates around its enactment, or to enlarge the description by analyzing and referring to the outside interests (lobbies) which may determine the terms of the debate. The lobbies rarely have an obviously political purpose or character; more commonly, they are built around strictly economic ends or seek some form of social amelioration (for instance, trades unions or employers' associations on the one hand, pressure groups for the abolition of hanging or the introduction of free medicine on the other). Yet because these lobbies need to work through their society's political machinery if they are to be successful, they themselves enter the political process and everything about them becomes relevant to the political historian.

The story of politics is essentially one of conflict, or at least of interaction: one man by himself, even as a member of a political society, cannot be political. Power has no meaning except insofar as it is exercised over others, contested with others, won from or lost to others. The history of politics is the history of men adjusting to one another and to their society, but also the history of societies coexisting in active contact—allying, falling apart, waging war, deceiving or aiding one another, jostling (not necessarily with hostile intent) and touching, but most definitely not isolated one from another. There is no politics without contact, and therefore no political history without a full understanding of the system within which the political elements (individuals or societal groupings) move into contact with one another.

For practical purposes, the present-day historian has his political units provided for him. A structure composed of essentially sovereign and separate states may not be the only one in which mankind can organize itself, but it happens to be the one that has prevailed through most of recorded history. Lesser units (provinces, regions, townships; guilds, private societies, professional associations) may sometimes have a history of the kind that attracts the political historian, but they should always be treated as embedded in the larger unit of a state if their own history is to make sense. As for the exceptionally large organisms which we call empires, and which at times have absorbed within themselves units previously and again after a while independent in themselves, they have virtually never been so all-embracing as to alter the general structure of coexistent statelike organizations. The Roman and Chinese empires may be regarded as having come near to this condition of eliminating the international dimension from politics, but in truth they did not: even they had to consider external relations with such powers as Persia and Tibet. Thanks to the enlargement of the known area of human activity, the largest empire of all, Great Britain's nineteenth-century expansion, manifestly never escaped from the need to manage its relations with other sufficiently equipollent organized societies. On the other hand, the ages when the structure of self-identified units collapsed have also been few. It is, for instance, arguable that to treat Europe from the collapse of the Carolingian empire to the twelfth century in terms of "states" is to distort the historical reality beyond the tolerable: terms like France, Italy, Germany, even England may have meant something in geography, but these entities clearly had no significance as politically identifiable socie-ties. Historians who, bemused by the nineteenth century, have treated them as states, have been anachronistic and misleading. This is true enough, but even in that situation visible units, often small and somewhat fuzzy round the edges, lived side by side and needed to consider their mutual relations. Throughout recorded history, however, times when organized societies, divided one from another, in-ternally coherent and externally unattached, form the raw material of political life have clearly predominated. Though our modern (and despite everything still prevalent) system of national states must not so readily be treated as the only possible system as perhaps it was by earlier generations of historians, only willful blindness to fact could pretend that it does not provide the clearest example of a very general human condition. Mankind has ordinarily lived in com-munities which were relatively small, organized in a com-prehensive power structure within themselves, and engaged in power relations with one another. Politics have always taken place on a stage set in this fashion; political history tells of the fortunes of power inside units of this type and of the fortunes of power between them.

It therefore follows that the political historian who wishes to understand and relate the history of his primary preoccu-pation needs to understand and relate the elements that produce given political structures in particular and ascer-tainable circumstances. He needs to study international sys-tems and domestic political situations. These matters have conventionally been assigned to specific categories of his-torical writing, and while it would be folly to work these classifications to death, it must be said that their use is help-ful inasmuch as it makes possible a clearer thinking about some of the forms that political history must take. The rela-tions between states consist either of negotiation or war; the internal structure of states depends on the manner in which power is made available and active. The political historian thus needs to attend to the special divisions of history which are called diplomatic and military on the one hand, constitutional and administrative on the other. While in their purest (exclusively descriptive) form these divisions, and especially the last two, may have an autonomous existence of their own, they are so very much concerned with explaining the context of political action that, in the real sense defined by the actual enterprise of writing history, they become subsidiary and partial definitions of political history itself. More marginally, perhaps, yet another form of historical study occupies a place of immediate concern to the political historian. If he is to do justice to the politics of an age, he needs to understand the ideas and ideals which in that age investigated and instigated action. This is the subject matter of what is conventionally called the history of political thought; it, too, at times becomes no more than a subdivision of political history, especially when it concerns itself with that difficult and tenuous subject, general thinking about politics. I therefore propose to consider the manner in which these subdivisions fold into the political historian's type of history. Since the services they render him depend entirely on the correctness of the manner in which they are practiced, I shall at the same time offer some constructive criticisms for their treatment. After that it will be possible to consider the major criticisms offered of the whole idea of writing political history.

2. Diplomatic and Military History

Ever since the study of history became professionalized in the nineteenth century, a large part of the product has concerned itself with what went on "in the chancelleries of Europe" (and elsewhere); a high proportion of all the historical writing done has been diplomatic history of a straightforward kind. By straightforward I mean that kind of history which unraveled and presented the negotiations of government (foreign policy) and got its information from the papers of ministries of external affairs. Policy-making assessments of the situation, instructions to representatives, despatches from them, memoranda of conversa-tions with the representatives of other powers, these formed the main supply of historical material to, for instance, the great Ranke and his school, as well as to generations of notable scholars of more recent years like C. K. Webster or Dexter Perkins. The whole idea was well summed up in the title given to the collection of documents produced in Germany after World War I, *die grosse Politik*—this kind of history deals with "great politics." When in the nineteenth century the archives of the powers were grad-ually opened to scholars, these were the materials which first attracted attention. They had the advantages of full-ness, of cohesion, of comprehensibility, and—since their authors pursued conscious ends—of rationality; it seemed sensible to consider the history of states as the history of negotiations among them.

That sort of history is under a cloud today, though it still gets written.[2] It certainly had (and has) some odd charac-teristics. First of all, its raw material is markedly limited and very much of a kind; it lacks the variety which better reflects the realities of life. The documents are all treaties, letters, and memoranda; they do not include such things as financial accounts, legal records, estate documents, last wills, the minutes of deliberative bodies or the records of legislation, to name a few of the things which preoccupy other historians. These are materials with very few tech-nical problems; anyone can read and understand them, at least at their face value. The criticisms which they need if their real meaning is to be elucidated is also relatively

straightforward, compounded of a common-sense skepticism vis-à-vis the motives of all politicians and a diligent
comparison of all the various documents bearing on a given
negotiation. Lack of variety is quite a serious drawback; the
"pure" diplomatic historian encounters too narrow a range
of the evidence which the past has left behind of its doings.
But the simplicity of the material has advantages in that it
can produce good results within its own terms: it is less
frustrating than most historical evidence, and diplomatic
history can at least be written.

Second, traditional diplomatic history moves in markedly
confined circles. What people did and thought comes to be
reduced to what people did and thought as diplomats. The
game is often enough compared to that of chess, and the
diplomatic historian does too often seem to be playing some
such checkerboard game. Not only do his actors apparently
exist only in the world of conference rooms and private
desks, but even such complex things as the interests of
nations, the motives which govern action, are derived solely
from "state papers," from some participant's reflections on
what he considers these notions to mean. English historians
of nineteenth-century diplomacy, for instance, are very
thoroughly aware of two such papers: the memorandum of
May 20, 1820 in which Lord Castlereagh defined "the
foundations of British policy," and that of 1907 in which
Sir Eyre Crowe propounded the fundamentals of English
policy toward the expansion of Germany. Both are, assuredly, remarkable papers, full of insight, cogently expressed, sensibly argued. They deserve very careful attention and are very helpful to the historian. But diplomatic
historians usually allow these papers to be self-sufficient:
not analyses of a situation or of attitudes which require to
be tested, but established situations and attitudes themselves.
They neither examine the views expressed further nor go
beyond the diplomatist's opinion to the events and people

whom he was trying to judge. In diplomatic history, proper respect for historical evidence frequently deteriorates into a form of idolatry offered to bits of paper.

Third, the heroes of this kind of history are very special people. They may, of course, include the familiar figures of general history—a Napoleon or Bismarck. But most of them are different: ministers of foreign affairs whom the general consciousness has mercifully forgotten, envoys and ambassadors, permanent officials in foreign offices. I remember, when I was an undergraduate reading history, that I became very familiar with such "great names" as Cardinal Fleury or Count Aehrenthal whose contribution to the past fortunes of mankind, not to speak of its well-being, really did not justify the attention paid to them. I knew all about Lord Stratford de Redclyffe, who in the middle of the nineteenth century dominated the diplomatic world of Istanbul, and nothing of Charles Darwin who lived at about the same time. If I had some understandable difficulty in distinguishing between Lords Clarendon and Granville, who made a mess of British foreign policy in the early 1870's, I nevertheless knew that history was about such men as these, and not about Siemens and Pasteur who at about the same time were helping to transform civilization in every one of its aspects. This kind of history cherishes a predilection for *éminences grises* like Père Joseph or Colonel House. Was that Lord Malmesbury who, as Sir Arthur Harris, handled English relations with France in the last days of the *ancien régime*, really such a towering figure as he has seemed in some accounts?[3] Surely, these were all worthy men, and some of them—a Castlereagh, perhaps, or a Palmerston—carried enough weight as persons and actors to justify the eminence which this kind of history assigned to them. But many more did not. American history, thanks to that country's long distrust of all international affairs, has thrown up fewer such spurious eminences; or rather, its spurious eminences are found more commonly in the parish-pump history of domestic affairs. In countries where diplomatic history dominated both the study and the teaching of the subject, some strange distortions of assessment occur monotonously. The diplomatic historian, like the people he studies, moves in a small circle of self-important men and takes them, inevitably, at their own valuation.

While the importance of international diplomacy and national foreign policy, together with the self-contained accessibility of the material and the attraction of working out restricted set problems, has given to diplomatic history of this "old-fashioned" kind altogether too large a share of historical production, the history of the other manner in which societies communicate—the history of war—has suffered from the very opposite defect. War has naturally always fascinated men interested in history, not only because it is so frequent, but also because it is so dreadful. Popular history attends to war all right: there is a neverending spate of books on warfare from the stone club to the hydrogen bomb. But professional historians have done very much less well by war. In both general and particular works of political history, the agonies of wars and battles rarely appear at any length comparable to the impact they had on the people of the day, and when they do appear they are far too frequently treated in a perfectly dead manner. A battle becomes a date, the conquest of a city merely the ending of a siege, numbers of casualties become numbers and cease to be casualties. And professional historians who specialize in the history of war are astonishingly few. Since so much of man's history is concerned with his efforts to kill others and avoid being killed by them, this fastidious attitude, though highly civilized, is also highly unrealistic. What lies behind it?

The two reasons usually advanced are contradictory, or perhaps complementary. On the one hand, many historians think the history of war and warfare too "simple": it poses no intellectual problems, no complications of research, no chance of generalizing about forces and patterns, no stimulating questions of motive, intrigue, or contemplation. It is all action, with such thought as there may be at a very primitive level. Thus it has nothing to offer to the searching intelligence and may be left to retired generals and journalists. There is a lot of misplaced arrogance and misunderstanding in the rejection of war as a proper subject for historical study. On the other hand, war is also seen as too messy and ill ordered. It is an aspect of human activity in which accident and chance operate to such a degree that no one can bring order into its description or employ the historian's cherished ability to analyze the event from an understanding of its prehistory. The simplicity and complexity of war are really treated as two sides of the same thing—its lack of intellectual challenge, its failure to accommodate to reason and give scope to that reason's powers.

Now there is something in this, though one would have thought that these very features would compel attention and create an intellectual fascination of its own. So drastic an event, which at the same time upsets so many of the ordinary circumstances of nonwarlike life, surely deserves the utmost in professional investigation; and, of course, a small number of very able men have seen the point and come to grips with it.[4] Nevertheless, most of what is written about war, even by practicing members of the profession, bears out the general opinion by being intellectually undemanding and unsatisfying. The odd thing is that the supposed qualities of war, which make it unattractive to the superior intellect, are manifestly also found in violent revolutions, which are also unpredictable, chancy, brutal, and haphazard. Yet revolutions do not lack their serious historians—far from it—even in England which has experienced markedly fewer of them than it has known wars. This suggests that the

stated objections to studying the history of war hide different real ones; and indeed, this is so.

In the first place, even good historians need a measure of
direct acquaintance with what they are about to investigate.
As human beings, they share a wide range of personal experiences with all mankind; as members of societies they
know what it is like to be governed, to be under power; as
members of institutions (universities) most of them know
what it is like to govern, to administer, to intrigue—in short,
to live something like the lives of the people who form the
staple components of political history.[5] Part, at least, of the
attraction of diplomatic history lies in the apparent identity
of its events with the lives of professors, sitting on committees, negotiating with one another and with external
powers (government departments, foundations, donors,
rival universities, even students). But experience of war is
rare among historians. This may be a strange thing to say
about three generations which have passed through two of
the worst wars in history, but it is true, especially when it is
remembered that the occasional historian with firsthand experience, like R. H. Tawney, was (with reason) totally re-
pelled rather than fascinated. Many of today's teachers of
history have indeed served in armies, navies, and air forces,
but few of them served in those areas where "normal" life
gave way to the special absurdities of war. The educational,
propagandist, administrative, and intelligence branches of
military organization do not supply the sort of experience
which makes war real to the participant. Even being
bombed in London or deprived of butter in California does
not necessarily tell what it was like to face the British
squares at Waterloo or line the trenches at Antietam. And
the generation of scholars now growing up is the first for a
long time in whose personal lives direct experience of war
has played no part at all.

At the same time, especially those who have had the

experience seem reluctant to take the history of warfare seriously. And this—the ultimate reason—arises from their distaste, their hatred for it. War is nasty and dreadful; to the liberal intelligences which predominate among historians it is nothing else. The waste, the brutality, the deaths and mutilations, the stupidity of leaders and petty selfishnesses of the led, quite dispose for them of the occasional heroism, the intenseness of life, the brilliance of thought and action, which, they quite admit, also exist. In all this they are right—right in their humane reactions, right as human beings. War is the breakdown of an essential human and social truth, and as such a peculiarly loathsome disease. But for that very reason they are wrong as historians to neglect its study. At the very least, if war is a disease, diagnosis of causes and possibly prescription of cures would seem to be a foremost task for the historian who (as so many do today) wants to assist his society by offering it advice. And it might also be thought that the very frequency of war throws doubt on its being a disease; at times at least it seems to have been a sufficiently normal condition to be treated as the obvious state of mankind. All this requires study and explanation. Yet historians turn away from it, often exploring its supposed causes or its economic consequences, but making no effort to understand or describe war itself. This they leave to the publicists, to military men (and though war may not be too serious a matter to be left to the soldiers, military history certainly is), and to the social scientists of the Rand Corporation, to men who either by obtuseness of feeling, intellectual equipment, or narrowness of vision are much less qualified than themselves to do justice to the phenomenon.

We thus find the paradox that in the study of the relationships among social units the unrealities of diplomacy have been treated with that fond assiduity which supposes itself concerned with reality, while the realities of war have (barring a few exceptions) been left out of the historian's picture of his world. The result has been that too many members of the profession, and too many of their pupils, have come to despise and neglect both forms of history: the one because they can see how it has been done, and the other because they do not see how it can be usefully done. This neglect has already had some quite serious consequences, for instance in the endeavors of certain political scientists to produce a science of international relations which passionately denies the value of the historical understanding and lives contentedly inside its own self-created models.[6] That the insufficiency of so much historical treatment may explain the contempt shown for it is no help; the alternative treatment is positively dangerous since it pretends to offer straight rules of conduct based not on experience or sense but on axioms and logical inference. Furthermore, the insufficiency of these branches of historical study is serious for the historian: good political history needs to have good diplomatic and military history behind it. Historians are supposed to provide an understanding of the past, its problems, and its actions. At most times, the governments whose fortunes it is the political historian's prime task to follow were preoccupied with problems of policy toward other governments—with the issues of the macrosystem within which they existed. It cannot be right that one should find so many works of history, from textbooks upward, in which foreign policy and relations are either pushed out of sight, or subordinated to the "more interesting" problems of internal affairs and the more "intellectual" concerns like economic explanation, or when treated at length reveal the unutterable tedium of writer and reader alike.[7]

What, therefore, we require are better forms of diplomatic and military history, or perhaps it would be fairer to say, more examples of the best form which practice has shown to be possible. The particular deficiencies of either genre must be remedied. The historian of foreign policy and diplomacy must realize that the systematic study of despatches is only the beginning of his work, that the negotiations he so carefully recounts are only the outward manifestation behind which lie realities of politics urgently calling for his investigation. He needs, for instance, to pay much greater attention to matters of trade and industry, and to forget that these supposedly "belong" to someone called the economic historian. He must, at least at times, leave the chancelleries and go among the people (the top people will usually do). Though he will not often have to mix very far down the social scale, by staying among the professional diplomats he will simply regurgitate their illusions, reproduce their highly specialized lives, and tell the story as they meant it to be told—unreally. Above all, he should never take their word for it when they plead public opinion or some other formless pressure in explanation of their actions: let him look into this.

A good example of the kind of thing required arises from the familiar, and difficult, problem of policy-making and the influences that play upon it. German historians, for instance, have been too prone to discover great policy-makers who devised a line of action and followed it through triumphantly. Not only have they endowed Bismarck with these qualities (who in measure had them) but they have ascribed them equally to someone like that weary cynic, the Marquess of Salisbury, who himself certainly knew better. Diplomatic history must get away from its predilection for either the great foreign secretary or the great conspirator (must lose its Bismarck and Holstein complexes) so as to discover where, how, by whom, and under whose influences policy was really being shaped. English historians have been prone to an even crasser error: that which supposes that foreign policy is made in response to "public opinion" or "Parliament," an error disseminated for purposes of propaganda or self-exculpation by diplomatists themselves. On the face of it, this view looks more profound and ranging than one which looks only at the diplomatic negotiations themselves, but it really embodies a failure to recognize what goes on in these matters. Thus A. J. P. Taylor could seriously suppose that a number of men whose loud protests against policy were consistently ignored really did more toward the creation of policy than the professionals;[8] R. W. Seton-Watson could speak of "weighty protests in Parliament which were even embodied in a formal address to the Crown" without noticing that the address in question was defeated by 224 votes to 64.[9] Necessary though it is to remember that politics play their part in diplomacy, the mechanics of the situation must be properly understood if devastating misjudgments are to be avoided. This is where the diplomatic historian's lack of acquaintance with non-diplomatic records has its worst effect. Thus an influential book of seemingly impeccable scholarship so completely misunderstood the nature of the materials which it was cataloguing that it came to drastically false conclusions regarding the relation between policy-making and parliamentary scrutiny.[10]

In short, diplomatic history must come out of its over-narrow and overspecialized professionalism. The history of war, on the other hand, must acquire professional standards and apply them to war itself, not only to the circumstances surrounding war. Something of virtue—rather dull virtue—has been introduced into the subject in the official histories of World War II, produced in the main by professional historians. The best of them is that produced under the aegis of the British Cabinet Office and edited by Sir James Butler, but the American and Australian series are also very respectable. Military historians need to combine the professional historian's well-established interest in the bringing about of war and its consequences with the professional soldier's interest in strategy, tactics, weapons, and so forth, and with the amateur's involvement in the fury, squalor, and romance of battles. There is really no need to suggest recipes for success: what is required is a renewed recognition among "real" historians that war itself and its attendant circumstances are central to human experience and therefore deserve the most exact and complete treatment that professional historiography can give to them.[11]

At any rate, further progress in political history in general depends, in the first instance, on a renovation in those branches of history that deal with the relations between states. They need to rethink themselves, acquire the sophistication which comes from asking more searching and more extensive questions, and enlarge the range of materials upon which they rely. Above all, they need to think of themselves as "real," as concerned with the actual, time-bound, and place-conditioned lives of men. Until this sort of work is done, the political history of multiunit complexes will stop at the point essentially reached a hundred years ago, perhaps at best acquiring new detail or doing a bit of meaningful rearranging here and there, but not discovering a deeper understanding. Until those traditional disciplines have shown what, properly renewed, they are capable of, political history will continue to seem inadequate and superficial exactly where it should be most sovereign, and its methods and concerns will be shouldered aside by socio-economic or ideological enquiries which, since they are not about power and rarely about people, do not tackle the subject at its proper core.

3. Constitutional and Administrative History

An understanding of the internal politics of states depends on an understanding of their organization: how power is distributed, rival claims reconciled, and functions exercised.

The way that men conduct themselves in politics is clearly influenced, sometimes laid down for them, by the rules of the society within which they move. If one is to make sense of a parliamentary opposition, one needs to know the rules of order which govern the assembly and determine the exact form that protest or resistance will take; if one wishes to explain the significance of legal actions, one must understand how the courts operate; if one wants to place the importance of taxation in politics, one must first learn about the resources and machinery available to a government. Examples of the disaster which attends upon failure to observe these obvious rules are legion; one will suffice. The historical reputation of Henry VII of England was for centuries based on the angry comments of chroniclers and contemporaries who called him a grasping miser, nor could historians get away from this judgment by attempting to evaluate these sources by trying to establish the motives of the commentators. They were further influenced by the fact that such documentary material as they knew seemed, on the face of it, to bear out the allegations of improper and rapacious exactions. In recent years, those concerned with this piece of history have done two things: they have greatly enlarged the area of the evidence studied, and they have endeavored to understand that evidence from an understanding of the processes which brought it into being. The result has been to contradict the surface appearance of the record and to introduce the reality of life into the discussion. Such technical terms as "process of outlawry" or "escheat of lands," which were once used to exemplify tyrannical action and to substantiate the traditional view, came to be seen as technicalities of the law which, when properly understood, deprived the king's doings of the air of willful illegality. Personality and policy changed before one's very eyes. The whole political history of this important reign will have to be rewritten in the light of better knowledge, but though the task is urgent it will, despite everything, have to wait upon better knowledge still.[12]

These problems of the internal structure of states are the province of those familiar subdivisions, constitutional and administrative history. The first deals with the organization which men apply to the ordering of their society, with the allocation of rights, privileges, and duties, and with the mechanism of the struggle for power. The second attends to the history of institutions and those who operate them, to the actual working of the machinery whose general layout and governing principles the first professes to study. The two are thus absolutely linked; and they are linked, too, in the mixed feelings of dislike they inspire. The dominant passions of the day are for social analysis, and there are more and more historians who think themselves insulted if one asks them to practice any other form of enquiry, especially one which confronts the social analyzer's splendid structures with awkward questions about his real understanding of the evidence or his precision in employing it. Thus administrative history in particular bears the stigma of being lowly and dull. Anyone, one understands, can do it, and it is the proper preserve of doctoral dissertations. All that, in some people's opinions, it seems to require is a stodgy willingness to read masses of often rather repulsive material and a flat ability to describe offices and office holders. When the work is done on the grand scale, as in T. F. Tout's six volumes of *Chapters in the Administrative History of Mediaeval England*,[13] it may evoke respect for the sheer industry and persistence displayed, but few will read the result and many will react to it with undisguised contempt for so much labor devoted to such dry matters.

Constitutional history, on the other hand, suffers from much the same drawbacks as diplomatic history. It was the chief pride of an earlier generation of historians who thought that they were studying the one type of history worth writing. In the heyday of the British constitution, when one society at least seemed to have solved the problem of how men may live peacefully together, it was axiomatic that the most useful thing the historian could do was to work out how this happy consummation had come about. In this way he would encourage proper pride in his own nation and help less fortunate societies to discover the answer for themselves. Non-British historians shared, on occasion, the passion for constitutional history (and more rarely the passion for the British constitution) because they wished to find out at least what was wrong, if anything was wrong, in the government of their own country. Everybody thought that a study of "the constitution" would prove self-sufficient in itself. The success of the United States in holding together a vast region without the weapons of despotism seemed linked with its possession of a formal constitution; and throughout the nineteenth century the making of national constitutions was a major industry, or at least a seemingly useful hobby, in most parts of the globe. The passage of time has dimmed these glories. The British empire is no more (unfortunately: its claims to constitutional excellence are even more apparent in retrospect than they were at the time), and though more communities than ever before use replicas of the English constitution, the outcome only demonstrates that this is not a sensible way to organize societies of such diverse and conflicting traditions. The American constitution is no longer regarded as capable of solving social problems to which it so often seems irrelevant, and the actual working of government in the United States is increasingly arousing the suspicion that 1787 achieved more mistakes than triumphs. At any rate, it is quite obvious, and quite true, that an understanding of constitutions, of the formal manner in which society is organized, is not enough for an understanding of that society's pathology; and the primacy of constitutional history has vanished with the trust once reposed in the constitutions studied.

The chief charges against constitutional history in both Britain and the United States are probably that it is unreal and that it is inescapably teleological. It is thought unreal because it deals with surface appearances and reverses the actual order of things. To the traditional constitutional historian, the arrangements that men made governed their history, whereas we now supposedly know that institutions are the product of social and individual histories: they have no meaning except in a context of social relationships, and to study them by themselves, as independently significant, is obtuse. The charge varies a little in the two countries. It has rather greater weight in the United States where traditional constitutional history too often meant the analysis of the Constitution and its Amendments, plus the manner in which court decisions altered or applied this body of rules. That is to say, it unquestionably used to tend toward a ritualistic kind of rigidity and toward taking far too little of life into account. The absence of a formal constitution has saved British historians from this fault, but their traditional predilection for turning the history of all government into the history of Parliament has had a similar limiting effect. A history whose chief ingredients are the privileges of the House of Commons or the details of franchise reform acts does look pretty thin and unreal today.

Moreover, the established conviction of historians that these respective constitutions were admirable—not perhaps perfect but definitely on the road to perfection—too often led them to write history with a predetermined end. With the decline of national self-confidence and the growth of a more sophisticated attitude to the past, both historians and their readers increasingly found this unsatisfactory. A strengthening conviction among historians that the past must be studied "for its own sake" rather than as a stage leading to the present combined with a general skepticism in the face of national self-praise to give this history a bad name. Earlier and rather simple assumptions of excellence suffered much damage as the social scientists applied their instruments to the study of historical societies; the realities of the political struggle, the selfishness of hitherto admired interests, the relativism stressed by social anthropologists, have all undermined traditional constitutional history. But since the general textbooks have limped a long way behind these more recent recognitions, as is their engaging habit, the subject has mostly continued to be taught in a strictly old-fashioned way. Particularly in the schools, but regrettably sometimes also at the universities, people still encounter a treatment which concentrates on such academic topics as the precedents for free speech in Parliament, the growth of ministerial responsibility,[14] the local government act of 1885, or the abstract principle of judicial review, as though no one has ever pointed out that these things happened in live circumstances, among and to people with specific (social, economic, and ideological) concerns and involved in power struggles. Dissatisfaction with this kind of history is fully justified.

However, this is not to say that the preoccupations of constitutional and administrative history are themselves pointless. On the contrary, the widening interests of the historian have made them more essential than ever. This is particularly true of those relatively novel researches into social structure which are now so popular. A massive work like Lawrence Stone's *The Crisis of the Aristocracy*[15] no doubt owes most of its achievement to solid work on the sources illuminated by the questions and techniques of the social scientists, but its conclusions would be ill based indeed if its author had not learned to understand the materials he was using. And those materials were produced by particular administrative processes within the framework of a particular system of government. Anyone, for instance, wishing to determine the wealth of Stone's aristocrats faces notorious technical problems in such matters as telling a mortgage from a sale or calculating indebtedness from bonds for debts which only a very thorough grasp of the administrative and legal organization of that society can solve. If such understanding is important to the social and economic historian, it is absolutely vital to the political historian. He wants to tell a story in which the actors employed specific instruments of action and operated—willingly or not—within a stated order of organized power. It must be quite obvious that this makes the history of government—administrative and constitutional history —an integral part of political history. But this integral part itself needs to reconsider its methods and purposes.

Of the two, administrative history is more basic, constitutional history more informative. The political historian needs first to be thoroughly acquainted with what happened and could happen in the ordinary running of affairs within the society that is his concern, and thus to understand the machinery which made possible the translation of power into action; only then is he able to tell the political story both accurately and in depth. If, to take an example, he wants to tell how the Tudors conducted their policy, he soon discovers that the apparent source of all action was the monarchs and that he must therefore establish the degree of freedom of action which they enjoyed. A traditional attention to the personalities in question and a traditional set of categories touching freedom and constraint are likely to persuade him that he is discoursing of a despotism. His ordinary materials—the letters from contemporaries in particular—are full of awed adulation for kings and queens; pamphlets and sermons seem to enjoin unquestioning obedience; familiar state trials and the like tell of the fate of opponents. Thus most studies of the period, at whatever level of knowledge or competence they may have been written, have always taken it for granted that the Tudor monarchs "did" all that was done by way of deciding and initiating action and that in general this was a form of rule by individual wills.

Yet that conclusion takes for granted two obvious questions which, once put, are liable to dissolve this whole well-entrenched interpretation. The questions which, though obvious, are rarely asked are these: how were decisions arrived at, and how were decisions carried into action? The first divides into two subquestions: who contributed to decision-making, and what conventions of thought and attitude conditioned it? The answers are still coming in from the products of fundamental research, but some important facts are already clear. To the first subquestion, the answer is a variety, not only of people but of institutions (Privy Council, Parliament, subordinate units of governmental power at the center and in the localities, even nongovernmental units of social influence based on status); to the second, a generally received framework of rights and duties embodied in the positive law of the realm, thought of as binding by everybody, the monarchs included. The second main question leads to a thorough study of the machinery of government and the changes made in it. From this arises not only knowledge of the precise mechanisms of government and the limitations they impose (for instance, the problem of publicizing a particular political intent), but also knowledge of the human and social limits upon action. In the particular case here used, study has so far augmented respect for the effective powers of government agencies (capable of both occasional large enterprises like the rapid secularization of monastic properties and continuous strenuous impact upon the nation), but it has also increasingly demonstrated that the exercise of power radiating outward depended over-whelmingly on the willing cooperation of a hierarchically organized society uncoerced by any physical sanctions. Thus a proper study of the subject, really assimilating the details which administrative and constitutional history of the more precise kind can contribute, has on the one hand infused reality into the notion that these were strong and effective governments, but has on the other hand so confused the simple traditional outlines of the picture and so severely qualified the independent powers of any individual (notably monarchs) to take decisions and engage in action—espe-cially, has so far reduced the operation of mere will in the story—that the notion of despotism has come to look very inadequate. The concept of a "Tudor Despotism" had its advantages: it made possible a first sorting of the scene and the kind of initial story from which advance toward subtler and better accounts becomes possible. But while it seemed to absolve the historian from asking difficult questions, pos-sibly without answers, it did so really by begging everyone of them. The real story is complicated and much more difficult to tell, but the fact that a particular way of doing a job is easy is no justification for adopting it.[16]

The necessity for good historians of government (admin-istration and constitution) is therefore plain; but what should we mean by good in this context? There is no need to stress the demands of accuracy and thoroughness: in all aspects of these kinds of history there is still a great deal to learn. In particular, administrative history of the ordinary sort continues to call for work. Every historian engaged on the political events and policies of governments in just about every country still keeps coming up against his own igno-rance on far too many occasions. How did they do it? What were the means at their disposal? For instance, I have been trying to puzzle out a minor but rather ramifying mystery

for years. It is known that in the sixteenth century criminals
tried, convicted, and sentenced for felonies and treasons on
not infrequent occasions got off by producing a pardon or
persuading the court of King's Bench that there had been a
technical irregularity in the indictment. The trial took place
anywhere in the kingdom; the happy end had to occur at
Westminster. How was it done? How, and even when, did
men of no social standing or influence at all succeed in post-
poning the carrying out of a sentence to be hanged? In the
process, I discovered (what does not appear to be widely
known) that the courts did not pronounce sentence until
moved to do so by the prosecution, after the jury had given
its verdict. In some instances, therefore, the prosecution may
have been willing to save a man, for whatever reason. In
others, it looks as though the judge intervened. But mostly I
have no idea, so far, what actually happened. Yet on the
correct understanding of these processes depend assessments of the savagery and effectiveness of the penal law, of
the incidence of crime, the purposes and efficiency of government, even in the last resort the whole nature of this
government whose own enemies (traitors) were tried by a
system that seems to have offered obscure loopholes to those
adjudged guilty and that at present we do not fully understand.

Of course, work goes on and knowledge accumulates.
Now and again, some book seems to offer all the answers;
though a supposedly exhaustive treatise can disappoint in
the most surprising way. Sir Robert Somerville has produced
700 pages on *The History of the Duchy of Lancaster* down
to 1601,[17] but he says not a word on the salary of the head
of that government department, information which is readily obtainable from the duchy accounts. Even so seemingly
exhaustive a handbook as R. Doucet's *Les Institutions de la
France au 16ᵉ siècle*[18] at times leaves the enquirer dissatis-
fied. This is not to blame two excellent books: merely to

indicate that the amount of serious work still to be done on often quite obvious questions remains enormous. In English history, especially from the later fifteenth century onward, the unsolved problems abound. The reasons are various. Sometimes the evidence does not exist, and the blank will forever remain unfilled. Occasionally the question does not exist: if, for instance, one asks (as people have asked) by what instruments English medieval governments managed to control the economy, there can be no answer because in fact they tried to do no such thing. (If the question is re-phrased to read "to control the flow of trade so as to be able to milk it for fiscal purposes," an answer is at once forth-coming.) In such cases, by demonstrating the erroneous assumptions behind a seemingly straightforward enquiry, the administrative historian provides the political historian with a necessary revision of large areas of his theme. But in most cases, the reason for the remaining problems is quite simply that no one has yet got round to tackling them. Thus it is only recently that we have had the first serious book on the English Court of Chancery as a working institu-tion, staffed by human beings and following an organized way of life.[19] Yet the Chancery is not only an obviously important institution through some five hundred years of English history and supplied with massive (not exhaustive) documentation; it has also often enough been written about, without deep study, from the point of view of the growth of equity or the conflicts of law courts, matters which are put into a very different light by this new and "real" study.

This example, however, reminds one why progress in this obviously needed direction has been so slow. Among histo-rians of government, constitutional history still predom-inates: especially, where the more "eminent" institutions are concerned, historians prefer to ask the more "elevated" questions. They would rather ask where an institution fits into the scheme of things, how it contributed to political

conflict (they love political conflict), or what theories and
ideas it embodied. The question, "How did it actually work?"
is liable to be treated as inferior; and those of us who tackle
it and have to point out that all those "elevated" answers
seem a long way removed from what actually happened are
regarded at best as spoilsports, more commonly as truly
wicked and horribly cynical.[20] I need not labor the point:
until it is known how an institution or system actually
worked and what its records actually mean, nothing else
can be said about it with any degree of confidence; and no
amount of past consensus, usually derived in the first place
from some biased and unsound contemporary view, can
make any difference to that. Professor Jones decided to take
the Chancery seriously and in the process found himself
compelled to miss out all sorts of well-entrenched commonplaces about its political role, its functions as an instrument
of the prerogative, its alleged quarrels with the common law
and common lawyers. Literally centuries of inherited learning were shown to rest on nothing more than some mis-
applied later events and the prejudiced opinions of some
individuals who had carried the day with historians. Not
every administrative historian will be able to do quite so
much demolition work in one book, but the chances are
always that he will come up with a correction of detail
which will have to reverberate through the standard accounts.

The English Parliament provides an outstanding example of what should not happen and what needs to be done.
Ever since English constitutional history came of age, in the
days of William Stubbs, Parliament formed its chief and
sometimes its sole subject. Acres of paper have been covered with analyses of its "growth" and development, with
discussions of its composition and membership, with high
theories about its place in the body politic. It does seem
quite incredible that there should be anything further to say.

Yet it would not be far wrong to assert that, at least before the nineteenth century and in measure even after, we know just about everything about Parliament except what it did and how it worked. When one asks the obvious first question of any part of its history, almost no answer comes forth: what went on and why? The Parliament produced legislation: just what happened to turn out this product? As soon as one tries to take one's stand inside the workings of the institution, one is over and over again left in the lurch by the libraries of books concerned with Parliament. They tell you all about this speech or that, but nothing about the pieces of paper and parchment, handled by live humans, which are the main reason for Parliament's existence. All sorts of points turn out to derive from general notions or unanalyzed convictions rather than from demonstrable knowledge. Parliament gets equated with the House of Commons; the Lords rarely put in an appearance, especially after the end of the Middle Ages; yet for centuries they were the men who dominated society and politics. The Commons, one suddenly realizes, get treated as a unit, not as the collection of individuals they were. Everything is judged from the assumption that Parliament, or the House of Commons, formed a "balance" in the constitution and behaved properly only when it was opposing the Crown; yet we all know that it was called into being by the Crown and unable to exist without it. The story is told without attention to the elementary fact that the people involved worked by and to rules, so that members are on the one hand credited with a freedom of behavior which they never enjoyed and on the other deprived of credit for the skills which enabled them to use the rules and machinery for identifiable purposes of their own. It may be said, after over a century of intensive study, that for the main part of its history Parliament remains essentially unknown because historians have not yet studied it administratively, as an institution rather than a constitutional symbol.

It has unfortunately to be said that recent developments in parliamentary history have hindered rather than helped. Sir Lewis Namier's obsession with the persons of individuals—his belief that the history of Parliament equals the history of individual members of the Commons—has resulted in the one major cooperative enterprise at present active in English historiography: the History of Parliament Trust which is attempting to write biographies of every man known to have sat in the Commons and then to draw statistically based conclusions about the behavior of the House. The Lords, once again, lie forgotten. Worse, the widespread researches of the team have been so exclusively directed to the one end that even for the Commons anything not to do with members—all evidence bearing on the organization, the staff, or the proceedings—has effectively been ignored. Worse still, the people involved in the enterprise seem likely to surrender to a mechanistic explanation of people's behavior and the lure of a single big question, the question of factional grouping (or party) in the House of Commons. The big debate about the nature of seventeenth- and eighteenth-century parties has paid attention to only one aspect of the day-to-day handling of business, and that the most rare to occur: voting behavior.[21] A collection of documentary extracts for the instruction of students and concerned with the organization of Parliament has nothing on procedure or proceedings, only on faction.[22] And it is sad to find that the latest and biggest life of Sir Robert Walpole, notoriously one of the ablest managers of the House of Commons who ever lived, gives the reader no help at all in understanding how he did it.[23] Too few historians seem to be fascinated by politics as something you do rather than something that enables your opinions to be given a party label.

This sort of thing cannot be right, even when the omission does not lead to plain error. Of course, the history of Parliament should not be reduced to a history of its procedure, but until that procedure is absolutely clear and known, everything else hangs in midair. What use, for instance, are discussions of the influence of the Commons or of individual members, until we are really sure about the information on which they might base their influence: how much they possessed, how it came to them, when it came to them, whether they had means freely to obtain what they wanted? Yet even for so supposedly well known a period as the last 120 years, we have no serious study of that basic problem; at best, there are journalistic repetitions of vague superficialities and demonstrable errors. This whole example of the English Parliament shows plainly that one of the really important tasks before us is to attend to the administration before we study the constitution; or to be more concerned with what was and how it worked before we attempt to answer such questions as what it meant. Nor have I any reason to think that this state of affairs is peculiar to English history. I have had occasion to seek out some such problems in the history of other European countries and met the familiar blank wall; and conversations with American historians have at least suggested that these sort of studies would not come amiss there, too.

This is not, however, a call for the merely mindless or mechanical analysis of administrative points. The real pleasures of research are often found in just such detailed work, for its own sake, but the historian must not lose himself entirely in it. For one thing, administration itself cannot be studied successfully in this way. The work was done by live men; the evidence is dead; the historian must restore life to it. This requires the kind of imagination which sees those people at work and applies the criterion of human possibility and human motive to materials which certainly at one time were closely involved with both but may very probably no longer demonstrate the fact. There are occasions when the evidence suggests what could not have been: for instance, that the magnates of early fifteenth-century England allowed the knights and burgesses in the Commons to dictate policy to them. At this point, the instructed imagination—a learned understanding of the social and political structure of the time—takes over to suggest that, in a system in which the formal initiative in raising grievances was accorded to the petitioning Commons rather than to the responding Lords, this appearance was bound to occur. However, it is equally unimaginative then to jump to the conclusion that the Commons were simply the Lords' "mouthpieces"; the real interaction between them was subtler and can be documented from the hard evidence once a rational comprehension of their mutual relations has been grasped.[24]

At this point, then, administrative history again becomes constitutional. Or rather, it should by now be apparent that there is not much point in keeping the two apart. The distinction is valuable so long as it forces the historian to think about institutions whose constitutional function—especially any share in constitutional conflict—is minimal, and inasmuch as it reminds him to begin by really understanding how they were organized and how they worked. But what we are talking about is in fact one theme: the nature and operation through changes in time of a system of government, taking that term in its widest sense to include all structures, at whatever level, created by the social need to provide for continuity of order, rule, and stability. Constitutional history of the traditional kind—whether it traces the modifications in the power structure of a society, or interprets the changes in a given constitution laid down in writing—must give way to the history of government in this comprehensive sense: how it was organized, how it worked or did not work, who operated it under what rules and restraints, how it affected those operated upon, what changed and when and how. (Alterations, even revolutions, in government and structure are naturally included: this is history, not sociology.) Thus treated and respected, the study will acquire a new depth and a new reality.

Beyond this, however, the often attacked unreality of constitutional history requires another remedy. Forms of government, and especially developments in them, derive from two fundamental sources: the needs of the society which they organize, and the momentum of their own traditions which in turn influence society. The second point is well taken care of by the sort of administrative approach already described. The first requires that the historian of government understand the inwardness of the society in question, the distribution of power within it, the elements that hold it together and those that force it apart, the relationship of classes or other subdivisions, the mystiques of social conviction, and above all, that for all these matters he should discern and understand their transformation through time. In themselves, issues of this kind—the sociological problems of history—are not the political historian's proper concern, and he must beware of getting too absorbed in them; but he cannot do without them. Even as he may demand of the social historian that he does not neglect or contradict the findings of political and constitutional history, so he must listen to his brother who will tell him of these structural issues. To the social historian, they are ends in themselves; to the political historian, they matter insofar as they affect his story of government and politics. Of course, the individual scholar neither can nor should divide himself so starkly into these categories, but since any man must in practice and of necessity make a choice of his primary interest, his preferred way of relating the facts of history, we are all rightly specialists this way or that. And if the historian has chosen to tell a political story, he will have to concentrate on that and borrow conclusions required for his understanding of politics from those who have chosen to study social structure and attitudes. If he tries to do everything, he is liable to forget some things of real importance; in the Namierite analysis of Parliament, for instance, the political problems of what happened and why are being submerged under the politically marginal analysis of who was related to whom, educated where, attached to what interest. Only: let us firmly adhere to the truth that all specialists are equal, only differentiated by their skill and ability, not by the manner of history which they prefer to practice.

It remains to speak of one form of historical study which is usually treated as being concerned with government and regarded as very close to constitutional history: the history of law. Well established though this way of looking at the past may be, it poses in fact some exceptionally difficult and little recognized problems and is rarely practiced at all well. This is so because it attracts, and is studied by, two very different sorts of people. Historians and lawyers may think that they are of a kind, but few intellectuals differ more markedly in their mental attitudes. Historians wish to understand the past by an empirical collecting of detail out of which they can shape an explanatory and explained story (or sometimes pattern), out of which in turn they can, if they will, extract tentative generalizations about human behavior. Lawyers are fundamentally concerned to discover general principles from which particular applications can be derived. Often, in fact, they work from fundamental rules to specific cases; this is particularly true of systems of law which center upon a developed jurisprudence, as do all those derived from Roman law. But even if, like those who practice the offsprings of the old English common law, they generally proceed by an accumulation of particular decisions and from these try to establish rules, they first of all have the search for a rule constantly in mind, and second, really seek to apply general concepts even to their law-making case law. This, which was true even of medieval lawyers, is the paramount principle in modern law. Essentially, therefore, historians are trained to induction and lawyers to deduction, nor do whatever reservations one may have about this definition do more than mildly blur the edges of its difference.

This distinction is further aggravated by a difference of purpose which can affect the study of what is essentially the same body of historical materials. The lawyer's interest in history is either purposeful or antiquarian, but only the first matters here; the private delights of antiquarianism have no larger significance and may be omitted from the analysis. When the interest is purposeful it is directed to the present, or to some substitute for the present—to the living law seen as the result of that law's past development. Lawyers are the most "whig" of historians. What matters is the law that has survived, in itself or by influencing developments, and therefore what matters is the meaning that a piece of the past has now. Lawyers' history seeks in the past an explanation of the present and attends to survival, not to past existence. By contrast, the historian, and especially the political historian, is concerned to understand the place and meaning of the law in its own day, as a piece of the past historical scene. Though the lawyer may well at times look at past law with a historian's eyes and the historian consider the growth of law through time, their essential attitudes are as I have described them, and are in conflict. I had this brought home to me once when I was asked for advice by a graduate student, himself a lawyer but anxious to think like a historian. He had decided to study an English court for which the first systematic evidence extant belongs to the reign of Elizabeth I. I found that I took it for granted that he would wish to investigate the early formative years in breadth and depth, covering a short period of history distinguished (in this case) by the fact that it contained the nonroutine part of his institution's history. I also found that his assigned adviser, one of the outstanding legal historians known to me and a lawyer trained, had taken it for granted that he would discuss the full 300 years of the court's history, so as to analyze its contribution to the general development of law and jurisdiction. The lawyer would think my preferred method pointless: antiquarian in the sense of contributing nothing to larger understanding. I should think this pointless because large conclusions would be drawn from what could not help but be a superficial study (by my standards as an institutional historian).

These differences ought to be better known in some quarters; a recognition that two people may talk quite differently, in all intellectual honesty, about the same complex of problems might help to avoid much misunderstanding and even abuse. The upshot is that from the political historian's point of view, lawyers' legal history is likely to be wrong, or at least unhelpful, or at the very least too limited. It simply does not ask his questions. Inasmuch as it treats the law in isolation—and this is a common fault quite distinct from a difference in approach—and fails to regard it as the emanation of a social situation (a situation toward which lawyers, to be sure, contribute creatively), it is also commonly too simple, even naive. On the other hand, law is an exceptionally technical subject, with a very technical vocabulary, and historians' legal history will therefore too often strike the lawyer as wrong—ignorant, mistaken, at the very least bemused and too simple in another sense of the word. Really good legal history, satisfying the demands of both practitioners, is so rare because the two have, without always becoming aware of it, asked for different things. Both parties share a deep and sincere admiration for F. W. Maitland, the one man who proved that the impossible could be done, but very little else.

Yet the history of the law presses upon the aware historian with an exceptional urgency. The rules by which people order their lives and possessions, and the operations by which they protect both, are so obviously central to all social organization that no one can seriously suppose he understands a system of government until he has grasped the law of the day.[25] Moreover, for a great stretch of history —the Middle Ages in the main, but also the two or three centuries surrounding them at either end—the materials produced by the law form a high proportion of the extant evidence. Though it may well yield information on many things that are neither legal nor jurisdictional, it cannot be properly understood or effectively used without a sound knowledge of the law and the courts which produced it. Thus the political historian needs always to know some legal history, and some political historians, working in certain fields, need to know a vast deal of it. Difficult or even repulsive though it may seem, it has to be tackled. But, once again, if it is to be useful to the writer of political history, he must seek it out with his own purposes in mind. That is to say, the lawyers' form of it is likely to have little to tell him directly, except that it may open a particular range of sources to his understanding. And not even that properly legal history written by historians, which treats the law in its setting of society and time-bound ideas, will quite do for him. The law that he wants to know is relevant to the organizing of the society whose political history he is writing, and to him this form of history is therefore an aid, not a major topic. If the government he studies attends to the making and enforcement and administration of the law (as they all do), he wants to enquire into that activity, not into the product; and if (as was often the case in the past) legal thinking dominated thinking about political relationships, he needs to understand the first because it illumines the second, but not otherwise. While constitutional and administrative history, being really only subordinate sections of his political preoccupations, is wholly part of his equipment, the history of law must be treated eclectically and with particular political questions in mind. Otherwise the political historian forgets his political purpose and gets sidetracked beyond hope of recovery. However, his interest so limited must be intense, for without a proper grasp of legal history, the history of institutions and the history of political action usually go terribly astray.

The problems of political history thus require a study of the structures which go to the making of politics; but these various specialist forms of history which have been discussed—diplomatic and military, constitutional and administrative and legal—need to be treated politically (that is, as contributing to the story of affairs) if they are to yield their reward. This reward consists essentially in that they give to the story the dimension of proper understanding and explanation. They help the story be correct, and they add to it by extending the study of politics into all the activities of man which touch the handling of power. Yet even this enlargement of the area is not enough. Men not only conduct their struggles for power and help themselves by organizing it for practical purposes; they also think about it.

4. *Political Thought*

The history of ideas is a branch of historical studies which has some very delicate and still unresolved problems of its own, with respect to its methods and concerns.[26] It belongs to the complex of investigations called intellectual history (*Geistesgeschichte*) which also includes such things as the history of science, of historiography, and possibly of art. This branch of the study investigates and analyzes the thinking of mankind as distinct from its doing and relies on formal writings (books and their lesser equivalents) as its source material, whereas other historians need to consider a very varied range of evidential matter. Its virtues and drawbacks are here not in question. What concerns the political historian is that in their deeds men have their thoughts, or at least their notions, and that these affect action. Some, at least, of the subject matter of intellectual history is relevant to him, but in ways noticeably different from those which ordinarily occur to the historian of ideas.

From the point of view of political history, ideas fall into two categories: those directly concerned with politics, the nature of the state and society and problems of reform on the one hand, and on the other hand those that affect action by creating a set of preconceived notions or a framework of thinking without themselves being about politics. The first form the content of the history of political thought, a well-established teaching subject and familiar to students of history all over the world. There can be few graduates in history who have not become acquainted with such names as Plato, Aristotle, Machiavelli, Rousseau, or Hegel, and quite frequently the acquaintance extends beyond the names. Historians of political thought have annexed many writers whose primary purpose was not the discussion of political society at all but who found that their interests— theological or economic or legal—involved them in understanding the political setting within which they wished to describe or reform their world. Thus St. Thomas Aquinas and Luther and Newman, Malthus and Keynes, Bracton and Grotius and Oliver Wendell Holmes, have all at times been treated as writers on politics. The problems of social organization and the use of power are so central to all human activity that this kind of overspilling is entirely justified. But it makes the work of the historian of political thought less straightforwardly useful to the historian of politics than the latter seems to understand. There are three pitfalls to note, all of them commonly encountered; this is quite apart from the existence of the dull sort of political history which assumes that ideas have no place in it at all. Such philistine error need not concern us here: we presuppose that we are speaking of intelligent political history.

The first danger arises from the facts about intellectual history already mentioned: that it treats of such ideas as have become embodied in formal writings. It is therefore preoccupied with the outstanding men, with those who think deep, analyze systematically, prognosticate or predict profoundly, and have had the time and energy to write. This is one form of the "great man" theory of history, not in itself necessarily a bad thing and one to which political historians themselves are often quite rightly prone, but it is limiting. The great men of intellectual history are rarely identical with the great men of political history: those who write and those who do—especially those who engage in the activities of power—are as a rule quite separate sets of men. Not only tastes and abilities, but even more basically the sheer pressures of time, account for what is surely obvious, but equally readily forgotten. Since historians themselves belong to the first category they are liable to revere its leading representatives; since men commonly admire the qualities they do not have, the leaders of the second category attract the historian's favor; and since nothing is more agreeable than to find in the admired object qualities and preoccupations which, after all, the admirer himself possesses, historians commonly accord too much respect to men of action who also write. Hence the remarkable overvaluing of such figures as Marcus Aurelius or Frederick II of Prussia both as authors and as politicians. The problem becomes particularly serious when men of action appear to display a reasoning intelligence in their accounts of their actions. Men like Julius Caesar, Cardinal Richelieu, or Abraham Lincoln not only managed to impose their version of history on posterity but also achieved status as thinkers which is allowed to reflect on their status as politicians, and vice versa. However critical a historian may be of his sources, he cannot escape from the fact that words speak more loudly than silence.

This first difficulty therefore means that the characters encountered in the two forms of historical investigation are, by rights, two quite separate groups of people. The textbook writer recognizes the fact by relegating Plato or Marx to a chapter on "intellectual developments," a device which has justly annoyed those historians to whom politics is the least interesting part of history. More specialist studies usually ignore the great men of the other discipline, so that the politics of fourth-century Athens or Victorian England can be recounted without reference to Aristotle or John Stuart Mill, while analyses of Greek political thought or nineteenth-century ideas can do quite happily without a word about Cleon or Gladstone. This is neither dishonest nor entirely false, but it remains very unsatisfactory. All these men, worthy of attention in themselves, lived within the same societies and shared experiences; the thought of the one and the action of the other cannot in common sense have been utterly segregated from one another.

Recognizing this, some historians fall into the second trap. They discover influences. Politicians and statesmen are often supposed to have acted or reacted in accord with some body of theory available to them.[27] Thomas Cromwell is made the first of a long line of Machiavellians—deliberate followers of *The Prince*—contrary to the known facts both of his acquaintance with Machiavelli and of his own political views;[28] George III is said to have followed precisely the specific (and remarkably pointless) instruction of Bolingbroke; Robespierre becomes the conscious agent of Rousseau; late nineteenth-century statesmen are seen as executing the prescriptions of the theorists of imperialism.

As quickly as one of these rash identifications is removed, more spring up in the works of historians determined to make action result from the reading of books. The error is threefold: it commonly overstates the direct effect of writings upon their readers, it ignores the possibility that both circumstances and the nature of the problem led both actor and writer to very similar conclusions, and it overrationalizes the springs of action. At its most egregious it discovers influence when every known fact suggests that the two parties could never have been acquainted, in person or on paper, as when Henry VII of England is supposed (perhaps was once supposed) to have learned the measures necessary for the restoration of royal power from the writings of Sir John Fortescue which he had no occasion even to encounter. It is at its most insidious when the actors themselves believe it or put it forward, as in the case of policies which the governments in question pretend to have derived direct from sacred writings, a case variously demonstrated by medieval Christian and Muslim societies or by the communist countries of modern Europe. For myself, I am always skeptical of the notion that a certain political action was directly inspired by some theoretical exposition, whether it is put forward by the actor himself or by a historian. Of course, being skeptical does not mean never believing it: but one wants real proof.

The third danger arises on the rare occasions when a leading theorist does for once achieve political power: his actions are then interpreted in the light of his writings. With the growing prominence of professors (especially of political science) in the councils of government in the West, and for a time in presidential chairs in the East, this problem may become serious for future historians; past and present ones encounter it less frequently. But there have been cases. Cicero in political action has commonly been treated as a set of books, speeches, and letters engaged in politics. Jefferson was for far too long regarded as the formal and consistent disciple of "Enlightenment," without regard to the situation in which he worked. Above all, Sir Thomas More has provided a field day for this sort of history. Because he wrote a striking book on politics (*Utopia*) in which he propounded a number of reforms, and because some fifteen years later he occupied high office, the fact that we are largely ignorant of what he did in his years as lord chancellor has been covered up with confident descriptions of his reforming activities based on his earlier ideas rather than any known doings. That he was actually preoccupied with very different matters and by that time wished to do nothing to upset the framework of society is only gradually coming to be realized.

Thus the way in which the history of political thought and its proponents commonly enters the work of political historians is triply unsatisfactory, which helps to explain why so much political history keeps clear of ideas altogether. The natural skepticism of men involved in understanding the murky complexities of what actually happened and confronted with the clarity of what reflection produces in clever men, unburdened by the difficulties of action, can go much too far; there is justice in the charge that Namier and his disciples have been overwilling to describe eighteenth-century politics as though none of the people involved ever had an idea in their heads beyond some immediate and usually financial interest. As the influence of the social sciences grows, the danger will also grow: thoughts and ideas are the last human activity to submit to the formulation of laws or to quantitative treatment, and since they will not accommodate themselves to the preferred methods they are best, and readily, discarded. One already sees the effect in those many studies on both sides of the Atlantic which analyze elections to representative assemblies by the methods of the psephologist only. The present ascendancy of behavioralists in all forms of the social sciences (especially in the United States) both reflects the desire to eliminate this variable from the equation (or "progression") and reinforces the conviction of so many political historians that what people thought—their intelligent speculation—matters very little and can be disregarded as just another conditioned reflex.

This, however, is a desperate surgery which mutilates the natural body. People do have ideas, even unpredictable ideas and ideas quite out of character, as the phrase goes; ideas do influence actions which then often go counter to what an analysis of manifest interest or the predictions of behavioralist theories would demand. The fact that most successful revolutionaries have come from those parts of society which the revolution attacked must surely present a warning; nor can it be reduced to obedient order by talking of reactions against a dominant situation or one's own interest. Why this or that man, this or that body of ideas, worked this way or that still remains a question to be answered, and it cannot be answered except on the understanding that people do think. The political historian must, therefore, concern himself with political ideas, but he must become thoroughly aware of the pitfalls and manage to skirt them. Some are easily avoided. The crude manifestations of the "influence" notion need never occur; at least, it should always be possible to demand explicit demonstration as well as an analysis of the way in which ideas both entered the mind and emerged into identifiable action. The historian can train himself not to overestimate the importance of men just because they have left writings behind. But none of this will draw the fullest possible benefit from a study of ideas.

To achieve this, the historian of politics must escape from the major preoccupation of the historian of ideas. The latter wants to know the exceptional, the novel, the brilliant. For him, as for all historians, history is a sequence of events worthy of study, but his events are the significant produc-

tions of writers. The political historian should seek the
ordinary and commonplace, that body of ideas that was
readily present to his main actors. He is less concerned with
Machiavelli than with the conventional reaction to Machiavelli. What Marx wrote in a newspaper is likely to be of less
pressing interest to him than what everybody else wrote in
newspapers. It is perfectly true that most people in action
operate by a reasonably coherent and conscious set of views
applied to the situation in hand; to put it another way, they
act under the influence of convictions, understandings,
prejudices and commonplaces, not as completely blank intelligences reacting to given circumstances in an abstract
vacuum. These collections of ideas vary enormously through
time. Thus most sixteenth-century statesmen, confronted
with, let us say, discontent among the lower orders, took
steps which responded not only to the threat posed to their
own security but also to certain inbred convictions about a
society ordered in hierarchies and structured by identifiable
legal rights and duties. Twentieth-century statesmen, facing
a similar situation and similarly concerned to avoid a threat
to their own interest, will find their resulting actions influenced by general convictions about society in which egali-
tarian notions and the primacy of economic solutions predominate. What alters stories in which very similar
preconditions exist are not only particular historical circumstances (events, organizations, machinery) but also bodies
of acquired ideas. For the political historian, a proper understanding of these ideas is, therefore, inescapably important,
especially if he is to avoid the error of supposing that the
acquired ideas of his own day have universal validity.

This does not mean that he should forget the outstanding thinkers but that he must give much more attention to
conventional thinkers—to pamphleteers, speech-makers,
propagandists, and writers of editorials. It also means that
for him the conventional area of political thought is not

enough. Other sectors of the history of ideas suddenly become prominent for an understanding, not of society as such
(not his real concern) but of society in political action (his
proper interest). For, as a rule, political thought—thought
about the nature, structure, and use of political power—
exists in pure form only in the major writings; and in action
it never works by itself. The political historian, endeavoring
to grasp the contents of minds whose deeds he is studying,
needs to know how men commonly thought about their
society and their world, and about their place in either.
Here again the areas of interest vary with time. No one
can understand the tenth or the sixteenth or even the nineteenth century without a reasonable hold on its theological
commonplaces—on what men thought God had done for
them or wanted from them. On the other hand, at other
times (as in the eighteenth or twentieth centuries) theological thought is very marginal to the actions of mankind; its
place is taken by such other systems of faith as political
ideology. Actually, the nineteenth century is very peculiar
in that for some people and countries theology remains cen-
trally important, while for others it plays no part at all; and
the historian must remember such things. Again, down to,
perhaps, the French Revolution, lawyers and their ideas
remain crucial for an understanding of the nature of the
state, and in those parts of the world where politicians still
usually train as lawyers (the United States and Canada, but
also in a different way the new countries of Africa), the
same truth still applies (a fact very readily forgotten by
English historians bred in a society in which law no longer
rules minds), though the legal thought in question is again
quite different from that which must be grasped for medieval or early-modern Europe. At the present day, however,
most men's minds everywhere react most instinctively with
an amalgam of socioeconomic convictions, knowledge of
which is therefore vital to an understanding of contempo-

rary politics; but earlier convictions belonging to the same category—for instance, the instinctive protectionism of the seventeenth century—also played a part, though less exclusive a part, in determining action. Since the early eighteenth century, the work of natural scientists has increasingly gone to the formation of the general mind, and the political historian who fails to allow for the mechanistic simplifications which Newtonian physics instilled in the lay mind of the eighteenth century, or for the pervasive effect of evolutionary doctrines upon every compartment of thought in the later nineteenth century, is missing important clarifications even in politics.

Thus to the political historian the history of ideas is a vital piece of equipment, but once again he must practice an eclecticism governed by his specialist needs. This means that he must concentrate first on those forms of thought which are most characteristic of his chosen time and place, and must, moreover, concentrate on their commonplace manifestations. That is to say, he runs seriously into the danger of wishing to understand a "climate of opinion" or even "the spirit of an age," two red rags (and rightly so) to all good bulls among political historians. And indeed, if he were to resort to such abstractions in order to explain, or rather to avoid explanation, he would stand condemned as a purveyor of pointless mystiques. Yet I maintain that he must nevertheless seek to understand precisely what is usually wrapped up vaguely in those dangerous two phrases. He must investigate and learn the body of ideas, reactions, preoccupations, and prejudices which are current in the society, and especially among the political leaders of the society, whose politics he is analyzing. When he has done so, he has found no explanation of action: every action needs explaining in terms of facts and evidence. What he has found are indications of likely action and especially limits to what is possible or probable. This body of ideas, which has been discussed, plays for him much the same part as does the analysis of social structure or of the machinery of government. They all go to make up the situation within which political action takes place; they are the landscape or stage on which things happen. They condition and possibly direct it, but they neither cause nor explain it.

Thus we come back to the political historian's primary concern. He wishes to tell the story of power in society—its acquisition, exercise, and transfer—and in order to do this rightly he needs to learn a good deal from historians who are conventionally thought of as practicing a different branch of history. He must, indeed, quite often engage in their practices and not confine himself to just learning from them. Some of those branches have in fact turned out to be specialized subdivisions of political history, specialized because they offer enough work to require full devotion and also because their subject matter is identifiably separate. This is true of the history of diplomacy, of war, of government, all of which are not only fundamental to political history but are simply part of it. Other branches are really rather cognate than incorporated: social and economic history, the history of law, the history of ideas. Unfortunately, the political historian's problem gets hardest just where he is most likely to be at the mercy of others. The incorporated "aspects" are worked on by men whose interests are his: here he may often safely rely on results and use them. The cognate "aspects" are not fundamentally concerned with his political preoccupations, and here he often wants to ask questions very different from those asked by the practitioners themselves. The political historian will be wise to remember the point. Otherwise he will either distort his own ends and tell a story of false emphases, or he will improperly neglect great ranges of human experience which, in their own way, also contribute to the story of politics.

NOTES

1. Trevor Wilson, *The Downfall of the Liberal Party* (London, 1966).

2. R. B. Wernham has recently tried, for instance, to revive the genre for the sixteenth century where it has rather languished. See *Before the Armada* (London, 1966). In recent history, where so much is still to do, it remains a popular method, so that, for instance, three scholarly books on one narrow theme could appear in one year: J. B. Kelly, *Britain and the Persian Gulf 1795–1880* (Oxford, 1968); Firuz Kazemzadeh, *Russia and Britain in Persia 1864–1914* (New Haven, 1968); Briton C. Busch, *Britain and the Persian Gulf* (Berkeley, California, 1968).

3. Cf. A. B. Cobban, *Ambassadors and Secret Agents* (London, 1954).

4. E.g., Piers Mackessy, *The War for America 1775–1783* (London, 1964); Michael Howard, *The Franco-Prussian War* (London, 1961). English and American historians in general seem willing to make an exception for naval warfare as somehow more respectable for their labors than war on land. Cf. J. P. W. Ehrman, *The Navy in the Wars of William III* (Cambridge, 1963); Arthur J. Marder, *From the Dreadnought to Scapa Flow: The Royal Navy in the Fisher Era* (4 vols., London, 1961, 1965, 1966, 1969).

5. Personal experience can be very important. I know myself that a year spent in political police work after World War II (in about as humble capacity as can be imagined) has given me permanent enlightenment about some of the essential realities of any society which no amount of imaginative groping could have taught as well.

6. Cf. J. W. Burton, *International Relations: A General Theory* (Cambridge, 1965), and *Systems, States, Diplomacy and Rules* (Cambridge, 1968).

7. Historians writing in English may be especially affected by the peculiarly Anglo-Saxon conviction (strongest in the United States in the nineteenth century, and in Britain in the twentieth) that "foreign affairs" do not really matter by comparison with real issues like liquor laws or welfare services. The drastic decline in the domestic standing of England's foreign secretary since 1964 reflects not only a change in the country's position but also an emotional withdrawal from outside contacts which in part represents a "popular" reaction to supposedly "aristocratic" preoccupations.

8. A. J. P. Taylor, *The Trouble-Makers* (London, 1957).

9. R. W. Seton-Watson, *Britain in Europe* (Cambridge, 1938), p. 24; *Parl. Debates* 10:1185–1235 (March 21, 1808: the address was lost after an all-night sitting).

10. Cf. S. Lambert, "A Century of Diplomatic Blue Books," *Hist. Journal* 10 (1967): 125ff. The book of this title, edited by H. M. V.

Temperley and Lillian Penson, appeared first in 1938 and continues to be treated as authoritative: e.g., G. Kitson Clark, *Guide to Research Students Working on Historical Subjects* (2nd ed., Cambridge, 1968), p. 55. The fact is that its assumption (that something can be learned from the manner in which diplomatic papers were laid before Parliament) is false.

11. An example of the sort of work that can be done is J. R. Hale's study of the art and practice of war in the fifteenth and sixteenth centuries, so far embodied only in his contributions to the *New Cambridge Modern History*, vols. 1–3. It has made a very different way of writing about the politics of those decades both possible and necessary, though no one has yet quite worked things out.

12. Cf. the controversy between G. R. Elton and J. P. Cooper: Elton, "Henry VII: Rapacity and Remorse," *Hist. Journal* 1 (1958): 21ff.; Cooper, "Henry VII's Last Years Reconsidered," *Hist. Journal* 2 (1959): 103ff.; Elton, "Henry VII; A Restatement," *Hist. Journal* 4 (1961): 1ff.

13. Manchester, 1928–1937.

14. A recent book—Clayton Roberts, *The Growth of Responsible Government in Stuart England* (Cambridge, 1966)—could have been written sixty years ago; it still deals with its subject as though politics and the realities of government did not exist.

15. Oxford, 1965.

16. This is a real case. Professor J. Hurstfield recently ("Was there a Tudor Despotism after all?" *Transactions of the Royal Historical Society* [1967], pp. 83ff.) attempted to reverse discussions of the problem. But he achieves his purpose by (1) applying absolute standards of "freedom" by which almost no government, and certainly no government of a region as large as England and Wales, has ever been anything but a despotism; (2) treating his examples of allegedly despotic action in the traditional vacuum; and (3) failing to ask the two questions suggested above.

17. London, 1953.

18. 2 vols., Paris, 1948.

19. W. J. Jones, *The Elizabethan Court of Chancery* (Oxford, 1967). The book explodes some cherished myths (for instance, touching the degree to which equity was free to vary from the common law, or the position of chancellor and court in the political struggle for "freedom"); and this can be very effective to historians stuck neck-deep in inherited concepts, a weakness to which legal historians are particularly prone. Cf. the review by Edith Henderson in *Journal of Modern History* 41 (1969): 231ff., which—so far as it is comprehensible, and much of it is thoroughly obscure—attacks the author for doing the right kind of job.

20. When some years ago I demonstrated that the famous "Form of Apology" produced in James I's first Parliament cannot be read as embodying the agreed views of the House but rather failed of acceptance there ("A High Road to Civil War?" *From the Renaissance to the Counter-Reformation*, ed. C. H. Carter [New York, 1965]), I was told angrily by a very eminent scholar that I had "removed one of the great constitutional documents from the

canon." Whether it should ever have been there in the first place did not seem to concern him.

21. Cf., e.g., the debate about the years 1688–1714 in R. Walcott, *English Politics in the Early Eighteenth Century* (Oxford, 1956)—a grotesque misnomer of a title; J. H. Plumb, *The Growth of Political Stability in England 1675–1725* (London, 1967); G. S. Holmes, *British Politics in the Age of Queen Anne* (London, 1967).

22. G. S. Holmes and W. A. Speck, *The Divided Society: Parliament and Politics in England 1694–1716* (London, 1967).

23. J. H. Plumb, *Sir Robert Walpole* (2 vols. so far: London, 1956, 1961).

24. Cf. my discussion of a prolonged debate in *The Body of the Whole Realm* (University of Virginia: Jamestown Foundation, 1969), p. 36ff.

25. By completely misunderstanding the sixteenth-century land law, R. H. Tawney produced a largely imaginary account of agrarian society and its troubles—imaginary but immensely influential. Cf. E. Kerridge, *Agrarian Problems in the Sixteenth Century and After* (London, 1969).

26. Cf. the interesting and critical discussion of method by Quentin Skinner, "Meaning and Understanding in the History of Ideas," *History and Theory* 8 (1969): 3ff.

27. The other side of the coin is more acceptable: the analysis which tries to discover how far a writer's theories arise out of his experience and the events of his time.

28. Cf. G. R. Elton, "The Political Creed of Thomas Cromwell," *Transactions of the Royal Historical Society* (1956), p. 69ff. The label was stuck on Cromwell by a personal enemy who misinterpreted a conversation.

CHAPTER 2

Criticism

However ancient and well established the writing of political history may be, it is at present under something of a cloud. At least, some professional historians incline to treat it as a rather old-fashioned and manifestly inadequate—even an uninteresting—form. Some think it too "easy": it requires none of the deep thinking of the philosopher, none of the sophisticated techniques of the social analyst, or the economist, no mathematical statistics, none of the equations and parameters with which the econometrist historian dazzles the understanding. Perhaps this kind of attitude need not detain us. If the charge against conventional political history is that it manages without all those graphs and tables, without the abstract vocabulary of the logician or the proliferating jargon of the sociologist, there would be little enough to denounce in it—certainly not the fact that it renders itself open to all. In actual fact, some political historians have been sufficiently brainwashed to try to dress up their accounts with these various adventitious aids, but it has to be said that analyses of voting behavior and such like are not being made to yield better or clearer answers so far by being written in figures and jargon rather than in English. These posturings apart, serious doubts about the validity of political history, or rather about the usefulness and sufficiency of a way of looking at history which concentrates on political events, do legitimately exist. They may be reduced to two propositions: (1) political history covers too small, narrow, and conventionally circumscribed a part of past human experience; and (2) even within its own terms and on its own territory it tackles its questions without sufficient depth and produces superficial answers.

Politics occupy a major role in the life of every society. They are the public existence of that society and the dynamic of its organizational experience. That makes politics important enough: but to whom? However advanced and sophisticated the society may be, only a part of its membership either will or can involve itself in these activities. Indeed, it is arguable that the proportion of the politically active decreases the more complex and advanced an organization becomes. Modern society, large in numbers, complicated in its needs, full of the details of life which require the services of the expert, has carried the principle of the division of labor even into its public life, in ways that more primitive communities did not. Thus even a lesser unit within society—a town or a village—nowadays commits its political activity at best to a selection from its membership, and at the national level the selection becomes very severe indeed. This is true, no matter what form a constitution may take—as true of democracies as of dictatorships. Neither the spread of power through bureaucracies, themselves in their own way involved in politics, nor the intermittent intervention of a democratic electorate really alters the fact that in the twentieth century the great majority of people are governed and have their politics conducted for them by a section of society, often a very small group. The recognition of this fact has lately led to a good deal of nostalgic complaining; much current "protest" takes its origin from people's feelings that they are unable to super-

intend their own lives and are subjected to processes controlled by remote, unknown, and seemingly alien persons.
The facts alleged are not untrue, though it remains a necessary qualification that a great many people do not in the
least want the burden and responsibility of governing. Besides, the complexities of a mass population living crowd-
edly at a standard of living extremely high by comparison
with past experiences (and determined to stay there) must
of necessity devolve the organization and conduct of affairs
upon a minority. Conditions of overorganization produce
bleatings for the simple life and personal fulfillment; conditions of anarchy bring shrill cries for order and discipline;
to the historian, the irresponsible outpourings of philosophers, publicists, and professional pundits are simply sad.

Curiously enough (because contrary to what is usually
true) those who think that such things were once better
arranged have a sort of point. The further removed from
civilized complexity a society may be, the more its political
activity can get distributed among its members. The people
of a medieval kingdom may have been divided into the
governing sort and those who did not govern, and the second
may have been the vast majority. But among the first—
those universally accepted as the part destined for rule—
the power to decide, act, or restrain was much more generally distributed than is the case in the governing part of a
modern state: the ruling "class" did "participate" as a whole.
And thanks to the relative independence of subsidiary units,
politics entered the lives even of the nongoverning sort. A
village in medieval England or France contained no one
who controlled the affairs of kings and bishops, but it did
run its own affairs in ways which would seem surprising to
its modern descendant, though echoes of the old order seem
still to survive in the more primitive conditions of the
American countryside. The matters that really concerned
the village—the rotation of crops, the rights to land, the

preservation of good order, and the punishment of offenders —were in large measure attended to by all the heads of households, bond or free, meeting in quite frequent assemblies and remarkable independence. And if one goes further back and looks at communities organized in tribes, political activity becomes even more the business of everyone, or at least of a very high proportion of all members. If one objection to political history is that it comprehends the doings of a minority only, it is at least possible to suppose that this form of history becomes more respectable the more historical it gets. And that is not altogether a bad defence of a form of *history*.

However, it remains essentially true that political history must deal with a restricted selection of all the people alive at a given moment. No matter how truly self-governing a community may be, a considerable part of the population is always left out of politics. The really young, sometimes the very old, nearly always all women, have hardly ever come into it. The genuine democracy of Athens excluded resident foreigners and slaves; the village court included no landless men or day laborers; the town council was restricted to the masters of crafts; even the tribe had its elders or headmen, and its nonparticipating and "alienated" elements. Politics do not form one of the human universals, one of the functions demanded for individual survival and therefore common to all men, like gaining a living or procreating the species. It is, in a sense inevitably, an elitist concern, and its history, however widely conceived, records the activities of an elite, if that term be taken to mean a specially selected group without connotations of general excellence or superiority. Nor are politics, so to speak, a full-time activity. Many of us do not want to engage in them, and even those who do may often reckon other matters to be more immediate or more important. Thus the question remains: how truly descriptive can a history be, how much intellectual or spiritual satisfaction can a history provide, which pays no regard to mankind's basic concerns and so many of its exceptional activities? Is it enough, is it even worthwhile, to analyze past politics and government, while ignoring the business of sowing and reaping, buying and selling, building and painting, singing and dancing, thinking and praying? Is it not true that, though all the ways of regarding the past may of necessity be partial, political history is exceptionally narrow in its interests, by the side of, for instance, economic or social history? Those who study and those who read include few who will ever engage in running a state or managing a war; should they be asked to read about the things they do not do rather than those they need to do? How "relevant" (to use the cant term) is political history?

Moreover, even if one agrees that the proportion of people involved in politics in the past was larger than it would be now, it must be admitted that this makes little enough difference to the history that either is written or can be written. The political activities of the village court are not only small beer and of limited interest; they are also not very well recorded. The history of public affairs—of the organization and use of power—does on the whole remain the history of "great men," of the leading few. Whether it concerns itself with kings and popes, or with political parties and politbureaus, it chronicles the specialized existence of special people; and the charge that it confines itself to a very limited part of the human experience must therefore be admitted to be essentially true.

Nor can it easily be denied that political history has too commonly treated of this experience at this surface level, without getting behind the public faces of men and events. Politics and government are, in a sense, always public events; those who engage in them are conscious of what they are doing; a narrative of these matters describes a relatively straightforward business. It may not always be possible to say exactly why a certain policy was undertaken or a law made, exactly when a piece of machinery was set up or how in every detail it worked, or exactly who took part in what; but in general these things can be established because they were the product of purpose and decisions, not circumstances and accident. Thus the political historian is liable to be content to record what appears, because for his purposes what appears also is, and he tells of actions and opinions as sufficient to themselves. Yet, the argument runs, this is to oversimplify, even to abstract historical events from their reality. Politics as an activity grow out of social circumstances and relationships, out of needs and conflicts themselves not necessarily political. Men's motives, so constantly cited in political history, are usually hidden, sometimes even to themselves. The letters, minutes of meetings, records of legislation, diplomatic despatches and appraisals of policy which form the staple material of the political historian are but a top-dressing on the mass of evidence which human existence leaves behind, and to write history out of them is to ignore the real interests and passions, the daily lives and personal concerns, the occupations and preoccupations which not only fill the nonpolitical existence of man but themselves lie behind politics and give them substance. An account of events which confines itself to political activity is superficial because it skates on the surface of life and contents itself with explanations which, since they are avowed and rational, must be partial and will be superficial.

The argument has weight, and certainly a great deal of the political history that has been written and is being written must plead guilty to a kind of self-contained single-mindedness which destroys the reality of the historical process. Nor does it much matter that other branches of historical study can be equally blinkered. When Thucydides recorded the conflicts in fifth-century Athens, he told a story in which the slave economy, fundamental in explaining the political behavior and potential of Athens, made no appearance. Accounts of the medieval struggle between empire and papacy rarely forget the problems of political aggrandizement or theological dispute, and are indeed only too likely to deviate into a lot of strictly intellectual history; but they are very superficial when they come to assess the situation of towns in the struggle, the sources of wealth, or even the motives of the contestants. Books about English or American political parties confine themselves to an analysis of the politicians engaged in them, to party organization and sometimes ideology; they tell of conflict and disputes as though only the hustings, the Parliament chamber, or the Capitol existed. Conventional political history, at any rate, preoccupied with narrative and guided by the evidence of deliberate intent, does very often limit its treatment of life to what lies on the surface.

A variant of this criticism accuses political history of being exceptionally "unscientific"—exceptionally impressionistic (a current term of abuse) and open to historian's bias. It lacks the quantifiable detail which allegedly provides sure foundations in social or economic history; it averts its eyes from the explanatory contributions to be made by medical or psychiatric science which might provide a control on the historian's ascription of motives or his understanding of his characters. He is just telling a tale—*his* tale—and cannot, or will not, check it against such certainties as graphs of price movements, tables of the yield of harvests, the models (empirically based, or so they say) of the sociologist, the scientific classification of human behavior—all the instruments and recognitions which, by abstracting universal elements and general statements from the particular, the personal and the accidental supply solid grounds for argument, comprehension, and proof. This sort of attack tends to underestimate the extent to which the quantified results may be absorbed into the political narrative; worse, it certainly overestimates and overworships the reliability of the graphs and tables produced by historians. Dull or implausible history does not become sound and useful history by having the print-out of a computer added in an appendix, but neither does dull and implausible history become exciting and convincing by being written in lively language and in disdain of such precise information as may be obtainable. For the moment, it will suffice to say that the opinion which equates quantifiability with depth and absence of figures with superficiality is less convincing than it likes to think.

Still, it remains perfectly true that there are senses in which political history suffers from treating too limited and too unimaginative a segment of past experience, and moreover from giving that segment a needlessly superficial treatment. Nor is it really to the point to enquire whether in this it differs from other topically defined ways of writing history: the faults of others do not justify one's own sins. On the other side, I do not want to devote much time to what is also unquestionably true: namely, that political history often gets despised because it deals with matters that politically apathetic or morally rebellious historians do not much care about. Politics can be "dirty" and "sordid"; indeed, in an age which has come to terms with both sex and money it looks likely to obtain a monopoly of those adjectives. At least, it will seem so to those who do not face the task of organizing the dynamics of power, inescapably present whether one likes dirtying one's hands (or even one's mind) with them. These personal tastes lie behind much of the preference for social history of both the simple ("daily life") and the complex (sociological) kinds, which is very popular at the moment. It is also true that some of those who dislike political, and especially constitutional, history, do so because it is thought old-fashioned. It is the thing that all the better-known historians used to practice; therefore, either it has obviously nothing new to say, or alternatively, to be up-to-date, the swinging historian had better look elsewhere. All these personal, understandable, but intellectually meaningless objections do exist—and do not signify. What does matter is whether the serious, and in considerable measure true, charge of superficiality must stand, and, if it stands, whether it makes the writing and reading of political history an inferior activity.

In the first place, let us take the charge that politics are the preoccupation of the few, that the main part of mankind takes little or no share in them, and that therefore the primacy of politics in the historical accounts cannot be justified. This is to observe majority rule where it really has no place. Political action, in the fullest sense of that word, is the main *activity* of all social bodies; they live only when engaged in it. I do not think that this point need be labored further. When we think of people *doing* something in society, we think of them as performing some species of political act. There is therefore every reason why the historian should address himself to the study and description of past political action: it remains the chief way of understanding what happened, even if the actors form a minority and even though it may not be the best way of discovering why anything happened. From this it follows that political history is bound to be the first kind of history to be written —the kind that has to be written before any other kind can. An account of what happened, of what was done, is alone able to provide the framework necessary for investigating other aspects of the past. History cannot be written at all without an accurate structure of chronology and a clear pattern of events arranged in datable sequence; and these depend on a study of society in action, on a study of politics. The deeds of kings and statesmen, of ministers and ambassadors, of soldiers and sailors may not be the most elevated deeds of which men are capable, but they are the only ones recorded with care and therefore form the only material from which a continuous series of events can be constructed.

There is even virtue in the oldest and most primitive form of political history, as for instance that form which treats English history as a succession of kings (good or bad, with dates of accession and death) because it offers a chain on which to arrange further knowledge. To be sound or valuable, all historical analysis or description of every kind —social structure, scientific invention, artistic achievement —must be placed in its temporal context; even a history of culture which uses such very vague terms as Georgian, Victorian, Edwardian is better than one which churns up "the past" with no attempt at all to allocate events to moments in time. I fear that one reads such social history often enough, even in good books which seem to think that a period of fifty or a hundred years is not too long to be treated as an undifferentiated unit of time. The historians in question would never make this mistake about their own day, but then time telescopes as one goes backward, and a millennium of Egypt seems like twenty years today. If the historian either omits politics or, thanks to the difficulties of evidence, can know but little of the politics of an age, he forgets the passage of time, perhaps the worst sin a historian can commit. "Roman Britain" looks like a single, continuous, barely changing thing in most books, described in analytical fashion (agriculture, population, villas, and that sort of thing); yet the generations who lived through this artificial construct outnumber those that divide us from the Pilgrim Fathers. History without chronology—that is, history without politics—perverts the fact of continuous change into a false picture of static situations succeeding one another, and political history is the necessary corrective for the common attitude which sees the past as a series of artificial vignettes, like scenes in a pageant. Political history is the cure for that false romanticism which pastes the past into an album.

Thus, political history must come before any other and has always done so. The study of history began as political history—the affairs of the great. It need not stop there, but unless it starts there, it will not start at all. The point is heavily reinforced by a technical peculiarity of historical study. The extant evidence overwhelmingly favors the writing of political history.

I have elsewhere discussed, at sufficient length, the relationship of historical writing with the evidence upon which it rests.[1]* What we can tell about the past depends entirely on what the past will tell us about itself. And of all past action or thought, politics—the organization and use of social power—have left behind the largest and the most systematic body of materials. In part this is because people have always recognized the importance of politics, have been fascinated by them, and have wanted to know; in part because political action, being self-conscious, has needed to create a memory for itself and has therefore produced a record. Thus the bias of the evidence is toward politics. Historical materials, subjected to a variety of questions, can yield answers of all kinds, but since the bulk of them is produced by political action they offer the fullest, most continuous, and most coherent answers to political questions. In this sense, political history is the easiest kind of history to write, not necessarily an overwhelming point in its favor but nevertheless one worth remembering, especially in view of the fact that in the writing of history "easy" means "made possible by the evidence" and "hard" means "forever obscure because we cannot know." The past evidently wishes to be known through its politics, and while we need not always humbly attend to all its wants, we still ought to respect them sufficiently to write political history.

* Notes for this chapter begin on p. 72.

Besides, the attitudes which despise political history as merely the record of the self-important or the contemptible "great" regard it as much less humanly valid than the social conditions of men, or hold it to be intellectually uninteresting because it does not get to the grass roots and cannot arrange itself in quantifiable impartiality, deserve themselves rather more knocking than they get. They are, not to mince words, childish and pretentious. Not to be interested in power and politics, past and present, is not a mature state of mind. Politics and political history rightly occupy so large a part of the historical bookshelf because they are fascinating. It is right for historians to want to know what went on in Council or Cabinet, who decided what, how wars broke out or ended or were averted, how a particular political trick was worked. These may be the actions of the few, but they affected the many. The lives of men may depend on the state of the harvest or the stock market, but they are guided and decided by the actions of the politically involved, despots or democracies, war lords or city fathers. Political history handles that part of the past which is not only best recorded and most fully known, but also, when all is said and done, the most important and the most absorbing. Even though only some men are its agents, all mankind is its subject matter.

There is one aspect of the reaction against political history which needs to be brought into the open. Many of those who profess to dislike or despise it do so because it seems to reduce history to a succession of imponderables, influenced by accident and by the personal. Any study of political events is likely to undermine the conviction that the fate of mankind is beyond its influence, is largely shaped by impersonal "forces"; it tends to encourage the view that things happened because individual and discoverable people did things or decided them. Now, no doubt, this can deteriorate into an anarchic, even mindless, conviction that history has no sort of meaning: when the whims or misunderstandings or even stomachaches of the moment can transform large situations, what virtue is there in history as a teacher and guide? Political history is the most undoctrinaire of historical studies, forever aware of all the contingencies and quite unwilling to establish patterns with a power to predict. To some temperaments, especially to idealist or visionary radical temperaments, this is intolerable. They want from history reassurance for the future; they want at least forecasts, but preferably the sort of prophecy which seems to rest on scientific assessment. Thus they would rather remove the accidental (individual) from history in order to discern the general, impersonal, and universal; and this activity is much more suitable in the study of economic or social or even intellectual history, forms of history which at times even demand such treatment. The details of political history stand uncomfortably in the way of such intellectualizing ambitions and severely inhibit hopes of prophetic success; it is another, and perhaps minor, drawback that they also undermine faith in the drastic revolutionary solution of problems by forever revealing the bloody failure of the most high-minded and idealistic intentions. Political history is likely to attract the skeptics, the particularizers, the conservatives, and its appeal to them lies in its masses of precise detail which continuously destroy overready generalization. By the same token it repels the generalizers, the radicals, and the believers, the men (of a religious temperament) who need proof that history is pointing somewhere, preferably in the direction they want to go. It follows that political history, more than any other form of historical study, humbles intellectual pride and teaches caution.

And, perhaps unfortunately, it teaches that men are differently great. The writer of political history forever discovers great men, and in our day this constitutes a charge against him. A perfectly proper recognition that history is not simply the record of outstanding personalities—outstanding in position or in personal qualities—has in this century of the pretty common man been perverted into a notion that history knows no great men at all and that individuals do not affect the fortunes of mankind. Or, alternatively, that any man seen to have done so must be cut down to size. Not many historians, perhaps, would frankly admit to holding such views, but at heart a good many do. Some tenaciously denigrate any established reputation they can find. Some, more subtly, ignore all individuals and bury them in social situations and movements. Marxists of all kinds—but they are by no means alone—especially abhor the notion that the scientific processes of history might be altogether turned by the accident of individual action. Insofar as such attitudes correct the simplistic assumptions of the old-fashioned political historian, on his knees before the thrones of kings, they are sensible and desirable. If they grow out of the conviction that by abstracting men from history the truth about man in history can be more readily discovered, they are misguided (even sometimes pernicious) but honorable. But where, as often enough, they are the product of envy and small-mindedness they are despicable. At this present time, a school of historians—and I mean historians, not only journalists—is developing that is devoted to pulling Winston Churchill off his pedestal. True enough, a pedestal is the last thing that Churchill would himself have wished to stand on, but the motives of his detractors have nothing to do with his egregious humanity. They cannot bear to think that any single man (and one who managed to enjoy war, at that) could have had the historical influence which this man did have. After all, they themselves could never have exercised such influence—and are not all men equal? When I meet a historian who cannot think that there have been great men, great men moreover in politics, I feel myself in the presence of a bad historian;

and there are times when I incline to judge all historians by their opinion of Winston Churchill—whether they can see that, no matter how much better the details, often damaging, of man and career become known, he still remains, quite simply, a great man.

Historians who deny that greatness in politics can exist, who refuse to find overwhelming personalities in history and cannot ever admire greatness in affairs, ought to look into their own hearts. Men who do not recognize and respect greatness have no business to write history. Naturally, greatness does not equal goodness, and goodness is worth finding too: but impersonal forces are the refuge of the feeble.

Thus the charge that political history does not deserve the very large place (even dominance) in historical study which it has traditionally occupied fails. The objection that it admits too small a section of mankind to its portals must be answered by saying that the activities of the few have been quite disproportionately important for all. The argument that there are better aspects of the past to study meets the powerful obstruction of the fact that the nature of historical evidence makes political history the most complete form of study, while the problem of writing history at all requires that the political side be known first. And the opinion which considers political history uninformative, limited, or dull is contradicted by the fact that this form of study teaches history's most valuable lessons: the infinite variety of men and their fates, the dehumanizing error of impersonal abstraction, and the potential of the human animal. One charge remains undisposed of. To be worthy of continued attention, political history should certainly not be superficial, ignorant of many aspects of life, or over-ready with simple and excessively rational explanations. It has admittedly been all these things much too often, nor has the fault been confined to the forgivably modest efforts of the textbook writer. What sort of political history should we write in this age of historical sophistication? Before that question can be tackled, it is necessary to consider the evidence available to the political historian, the use he can make of it, and the weapons he has at his disposal for articulating the story.

NOTE

1. G. R. Elton, *The Practice of History* (London and New York, 1967), pp. 9, 58ff., 77ff.

CHAPTER 3

Evidence

All forms of historical writing need to consider all forms of historical evidence, but the nature of the enquiry itself directs the main choice of materials, even as the availability of materials can direct the choice of enquiry. It is here that the primacy of political history takes its origin. However agreeable and even desirable it may be to study all aspects of the past, nearly always the evidence is fullest for the study of political events. The one complete exception to this is prehistory. Political history depends on the record, on the written word, and before such record exists political history exists, at best, in the most fragmentary way. Archaeologists rarely contribute significantly to political history. They may help if they uncover written evidence, as in inscriptions; and their discoveries can sometimes display an unknown political event (the conquest or destruction of a city, and such like) or at least elaborate or date one that was already known. In general, however, prehistory is more likely to be social history, the history of a culture, able to tell how people lived or migrated or (sometimes) thought about their world, but not able to equip those people with a history of events through time or of individuals at work in that culture. On the other hand, once one enters the world of the written word, the best documented part of the story is unquestionably that which deals with the creation, organization, use, and loss of power in human society. Even so, the evidence will determine what kind of political history can be written, and it also poses crucial problems of various sorts, depending on the type of evidence it is.

The materials of political history divide into narratives giving an account of events, into records of the events themselves, and into comment and reflection upon the events. In addition there is, subsidiary to the main classes, the material relevant to the subsidiary structures of political history—the records of government, institutions, law, and finance, not themselves directly descriptive of the political events but essential to an understanding and proper evaluation of it.

No historian depends more than the political historian on previous accounts of the events that he is trying to disentangle. Since he needs to construct an accurate chronological framework, he needs to establish dateable occurrences; and he finds these first of all in earlier attempts to do the same thing. Up to a point, he has to rely on earlier practitioners of his own trade, though in this respect his needs vary with his subject. The historian of relatively recent times neither does nor should construct his history out of the work of other historians. To him they are "secondary" authorities—which is to say, no authorities at all—and he should never use them without going back to the sources from which they learned the history they have written.[1]*
But for long stretches of human history, those original sources are now lost. The history of ancient Greece or Rome would not exist at all without the surviving works of ancient Greek or Roman writers, and whatever additional aid may come from epigraphy, numismatics, archaeology, papyrology, and so forth, the ancient historians remain far and away the biggest part of the evidence now available.
* Notes for this chapter begin on p. 109.

With only a little modification, the same truth applies to Byzantine history, the European middle ages before about the year 1000, or the history of ancient China, though this last is assisted by the documentary collections made by official historians.

However, not all narrative accounts are strictly historical, written by historians trying to tell the story of events, whether they are contemporary to the events described (like Thucydides, Caesar, or the valuable parts of most medieval chronicles) or live after the event (Polybius, Livy, Bede). Current narratives with no historical purpose can form a main part of the political historian's equipment. Thus newsletters and newspapers can often provide him with the first outline of his story, and this is material of growing importance from the seventeenth century onward. Political pamphlets or personal apologias can contain narratives of the history of the day, as can diaries or memoirs or similar private material.

That is to say, the constructed narratives which are the first section of the evidence for political history fall into two categories: historians' writings, and the writings of non-historians (people not *intending* to write history). Both pose problems of use and interpretation, but the first thing to stress about them is that they are usually quite plentiful, at least for the history of Europe and European-type civilizations from the beginning of the second millennium of our era. It is therefore no wonder that until fairly recently political history used to be written very largely out of them. The story of the medieval European communities was, until less than two centuries ago, essentially the story as told by their own chroniclers, rehashed in part, often no more than put together by ironing out differences and disagreements among them, and at times devoid even of such simple forms of historical criticism. The Anglo-Saxon conquest of Britain was best told by repeating what Bede had said.

The history of Charlemagne came from Einhard and that of Barbarossa from Otto of Freysing. The Hundred Years' War equalled Froissart (plus a few other chroniclers). But even when materials got more plentiful and varied, the hold established by the old narratives did not slacken. The English dynastic wars of the fifteenth century were always described and analyzed in the terms created by the Tudor chroniclers; the constitutional battles of the seventeenth fell firmly into the mould established by Clarendon and other contemporary observers. Other countries provide sufficient examples of the same sort of thing. Even the history of the French Revolution was, for some fifty years after the event, really written out of the newspapers diversified by contemporary narratives, especially the many and very unreliable memoirs of the time.

The reason for this endurance of narrative accounts— an endurance still painfully obvious in too many standard textbooks of today—is not hard to understand. Making sense of the jumble of events in such a way that a story can be told is never an easy task, and the temptation to accept somebody else's successful achievement is therefore strong. Besides, the old narratives not only hung together but were often very good and sometimes very right; the instruments with which to criticize and reorganize them, even where they existed, were difficult, technical, and often only confusing;[2] trained historians are cautious and distrust what may look like no more than frivolous attempts at revision, designed to attract attention to the writer. Thus, though inside the established story one could dispute and reconsider, the main lines of story and interpretation were handed down from generation to generation. And even though a good many legends—both imaginary tales and false views—thus got well entrenched, behind the practice lay a sensible recognition that this earlier work was not to be ignored and that it offered, inevitably, the first start at sorting the events of the past into intelligible history. The reaction against this kind of writing, necessary and indeed urgent as it became, has not always been pure gain. When, for instance, the wealth of medieval documentary material came to be revealed in the last century, chronicles fell into needless disfavor, and today too many professional historians evince an exclusive devotion to the document (preferably the unprinted document) which is as dubious as the earlier neglect of it. Part, at least, of the present contempt for political history and a very general inability among historians to write convincing narrative stem from the acquired conviction that narrative sources are too jejune and muddled to deserve attention.

Attention they should have, but it must be careful. The trouble with all narrative sources is that they infuse an exceptional amount of the purely personal element into the historical material. Whether histories, chronicles, or newspaper reports, they are specifically constructed for a purpose and allow another human being to intervene between the record of the event and the historian. Thus they need criticism or assessment before they can be used, and this assessment should be governed by two pairs of criteria. It matters whether the account is by a historian trying to convey an understanding of the past, or by someone not a historian serving other purposes (self-defense, partisan accusation, and so on); and it matters whether the writer was contemporary with the events described or was himself using some historical techniques on events through which he had not lived. Those points once established, the questions which must be asked are these: what could the writer have known, what was he trying to do, what can be established about his personal competence and opinions? By asking these questions, we can discover not only the reliability of the facts and interpretations offered, but also the depth and comprehensiveness of the account.

In practice, the last of these three questions, which on the face of it seems the most difficult, is really the easiest to answer. A good many books about history like, these days, to stress that every historian, compelled to discharge his task by a purposeful selection and linking of past events and thoughts, contributes to the product not only some personal elements (bias, prejudice, specific interest, specific ability) but also the socially and temporally conditioned intellectual instrument which is his mind. Every historian who has ever done a serious piece of research knows that there is much less in these superficially convincing charges than the champions of relativity would think. Nevertheless, it is true that in trying to criticize received narrative histories and their like, the historian must understand both the social conditioning and the personal qualities of the man who produced this evidence for him. If he is any sort of historian at all, he will know enough about the body of time-bound conventions which lie behind the mind of his author and will instinctively remember that interpretations may derive from attitudes no longer commonplace: as when the sixteenth-century chronicler Polydore Vergil expressed his pained astonishment at the fact that it was especially the wealthy and eminent who suffered Henry VII's attacks on their pockets. Nor are the personal peculiarities of such writers particularly hard to discover. The personal or political bias of historian or journalist or memorialist is as a rule apparent enough, even inescapable, and can be allowed for, and his range and competence may emerge from internal evidence or a comparison with others. His accuracy can often be checked against documentary evidence, though it should be remembered that accuracy is not a constant, being affected both by occasional carelessness and by prejudice. Dr. Johnson's notorious remark that in his parliamentary reporting he took good care not to let the Whig dogs have the best of it reminds us that a man may be entirely reliable if the evidence before him suits his book and altogether less satisfactory when it works against his desires. But these assessable personal points do not usually pose anything like the difficulties which some people seem to think they do. Anyone in doubt might like to take one of the many booklets that treat of some historical problem by means of extracts from writers who have devoted space to it. The editors usually provide some personal details and are careful to choose passages which, in the interpretation of the historical evidence at least, are in conflict. Then let him honestly consider the grounds of the differences and see whether he really supposes that they lie in the differences of the personalities involved. He will, I think, have to conclude that what really causes historians to disagree are such things as varying attainments of knowledge, degrees of penetrative intelligence, the line of approach to a question (which as often as not is guided by some accident in the historian's career rather than determined by his personal or cultural peculiarities), willingness to speculate or insistence to stay with the strictly knowable. That is, they differ as historians, not as human beings. By all means, as they say, "study the historian behind the history," but let it be recognized that a knowledge of the historian teaches no history and that the history written can only in small measure be assessed from knowledge of the historian.

The other questions are more difficult. It is important to know how well informed a previous account may be, and one should investigate an author's sources, whether he is a historian drawing the matter out of yet earlier stories or a reporter relating what he sees or hears. Modern historians give (or are supposed to give) their sources, and while the older historians were less systematic about this, they do often indicate a good deal. The Tudor chronicler Hall prefaced his work with a bibliography. Medieval chroniclers and ancient historians often cite in the text or produce warranty for specific statements. Nevertheless, this question rarely gets a fully satisfactory answer, especially when the account in question is by a contemporary. Who can tell what a man heard or learned in his lifetime? Worse, who can know what fact, obvious to the later historian equipped with access to the materials produced by the political process, remained quite unknown to the onlooker at the time, even if he was a participant in the event? These are problems as complex for the present day as for any past period of history. The study of any newspaper file can quickly show that the confident accounts of one day may be thoroughly demolished on another by the revelation of fresh detail, detail in existence but not known on the earlier occasion. Filling in the living observer's deficiencies from evidence of which he was unaware is one of the most commonplace activities of the working historian, but he needs to be careful not to get mechanical about it: the deficient picture not only has gaps but because of these gaps may be entirely misleading, and the completed picture should not be what was first found with a few patches here and there. At the same time, people sometimes know things which surprise: witness the medieval writers, stuck for life in some monastery, yet aware, through letters and the tales of visitors, of so much more of the day's events, distant or near, than the uninstructed modern reader might suppose. At any rate, while the historian need not waste long hours over his source's personality or conditioned responses, he should go very carefully into the question of his source's information; for in this way he will be best able to assess both the reliability and completeness of that information with any confidence.

As for the purposes of the piece of writing before him, these face him with two separate problems. One is, as it were, universal. The writer intended some purpose by his writing which is apparent and is bound to influence the product, and it is one which could be present at any time. He wished to record the events of the day (chronicles, newspapers, diaries), or to compose an account of the past before his day (histories), or to set down what he remembered (memoirs, autobiographies). All these purposes determine exactly how the stuff gets treated, how much self-justification there may be, what line is taken on controversial issues. Assessment can start from the known and patent purpose. More difficult is the problem of the non-universal purpose, the conventions, attitudes, and ambitions which may govern writing of this sort in different places and at different times. Even in so seemingly standardized a thing as newspaper reporting, the framework of intent may differ widely. There are obvious differences between local and national newspapers which, though obvious, must be allowed for; but there are as marked and much less obvious differences between countries and ages. Anyone who has ever looked at English, American, French, and German newspapers, all of the same day, side by side, will at once discover how different the conventional rules are in every country about what gets reported and how; and a similar experience awaits the man who compares the pages of the London *Times* in 1869 and 1969. The differences involve much more than different emphases determined by locality; they are differences in what may fairly be called social and cultural ethos. The problem becomes more serious the further away one goes from one's own local conventions. What different ages and regions regard as important or worthy of record or publishable depends on a whole set of notions—social, intellectual, religious—which need to be understood. The preferences and tastes of other historians may reveal a good deal about the society for which they wrote, but in turn they are governed by the preferences and tastes of that society, and where political history is concerned, the displayed social ethos matters less than the limitation it imposes on what will get into the record. In medieval writers, we look in vain for the economic analysis or the concern with the insignificant which are commonplace in modern accounts, even as in contemporary writing we get little of the lengthy description of feasts and ceremonies which seemed vitally important at other times. The deficiencies of the narrative sources do not mean that the things omitted or underplayed did not take place; the historian needs to ascertain what is likely to be habitually absent from the account if he is to do justice to what is there.

All this amounts to saying that, on the one hand, narrative sources of this kind must not be taken at face value, but that, on the other, the criteria for judging them should be precise and discriminating. To believe without cause is no worse than to disbelieve without reason, and neither is necessary. In practice, this work of assessment has been largely done, at least in European history, for those ages that depend heavily on this type of evidence. Herodotus and Thucydides, Bede and Einhard have been pored over to good purpose. Even some of the later medieval historians have been thoroughly studied from this point of view, though much remains to be done there. The work is nearly all to do for the historical writers and memorialists of more recent time—though of course there are some splendid exceptions[3]—and some hero could gain great merit by systematically teaching the principles of scholarly editing to historians of the more modern period. This applies, by the way, quite as much to documentary material as to narrative sources, and there are far more poor editions of the first than of the second.[4] We badly need a good study of the use of the newspaper in all its forms. Historians do use it, and often well, but too often also they seem to grope in a maze, content with a hit-and-miss method which has little to recommend it in the exploitation of this important source. Unhappily, it is often the summaries and researches of others which direct later comers in their choice of material. This is one department of historical evidence which urgently demands the attention of the systematizer.

Narrative sources thus are neither so straightforward as they are made to appear by the fact that they are constructed and offer a ready scheme for telling the story, nor are they so inadequate as some historians, bemused by the neutrality of the record and the seeming unreliability of any personal account, like to think. They give the political historian his start, as anyone can testify who has ever tried to tell however brief a story without a predecessor's assistance. But they are only a start, and they have been discussed here at such length because intending historians do not nowadays get nearly as much guidance for them as they do for other types of material. Nevertheless, both the real problems and the real possibilities of good political history cluster round the second category of materials, the records of the events themselves.

Whatever people do (and a great deal of what they think) is liable to leave a record behind, and these results of what people do and think and intend and make mistakes about are the main bulk of the political historian's material. Bulk is the right word, for in whatever period he may work he will find the quantity of these records large, at times unmanageably enormous. Political action, being of all actions the most self-conscious, reaches the record more systematically and more plentifully than all other human activities, which, as I have said, is one good reason why political history has always been the first to be written. However, plentiful though these materials may be, they rarely succeed in satisfying the historian's hunger. Bulk does not necessarily equal usefulness. Nearly always vital parts of the evidence are missing (lost or never created): legitimate and weighty questions fail to receive answers. This is true even for very recent times which are otherwise beset by the historian's other difficulty, the sheer mass of the stuff to be worked through. The telephone has removed areas of deliberation and action from the record which at earlier times can often be found documented. Furthermore, even when the record is full and manifold, these are materials that pose serious and often highly technical problems before something like the truth can be extracted from them. The political historian deals with events in which personal prejudice, bias, the endeavor to cover up incompetence or crime, and plain lies play an exceptionally large part. Even as his sort of history is more human than most, so his materials embody the weaknesses, pretensions, and devices of man more fully than do those, say, of social or economic history. Unquantifiable history is more subtle than quantifiable, more variable and more contingent; the historian coping with these problems and materials needs to be subtle, too, and exceptionally alert in interpreting his records. At the same time, it should be said once more that record materials are commonly unaffected in any meaningful way by the "culture-structure" in which they arise, though even some historians, unfamiliar with them, can suppose differently.[5]

The records of political history are classified by the stages of action to which they belong into four distinct groups. Action presupposes contemplation, consideration, assessment, and planning; it requires a choice between rival possibilities; it has results and consequences embodied in events; and it produces reaction, either counteraction or opinion (reflection) upon action. The records therefore divide into those of discussion, decision, consequences, and reaction, and each group has its own characteristics.

By records of discussion I mean the materials produced by the preliminary investigation which precedes action. These may arise from the deliberate initiative of the political agent, or they may consist of unsolicited stimuli such as reports on a situation, pressure from individuals or organized interests, a man's reading of the constellation of events. To take the second first: these are obviously a very mixed bunch. Anyone seeking action by another, or merely without intent stirring another into action, can achieve the intended or unintended end directly or indirectly by word of mouth or more permanent means, obscurely or openly. The chief documentary types which this category includes are letters (appeals, reports, despatches, information) and representations (formal appeals, petitions, protests). Understanding them correctly involves, on the one hand, an analysis of the document in its own right and on the other an analysis of its context as given by the fact that it produced, or led to, or may have led to, certain further action. Insofar as the document itself is concerned, one wants to know who wrote it and why, to whom it was addressed, how formal (or informal) it was, in short, what real purpose it embodied. These are relatively simple things, though this does not mean that they always find an answer. The contextual questions center on asking what relation it had to the next stage of action (decision) and, if it had any, how effective it was.

Here the pitfalls yawn wide, and historians' predilection for fitting everything into a significant or intelligible account can produce disastrous results, especially when assisted by the fact that a good many historians, faced with the difficulty of writing history at all, do not think very clearly. It is very often possible to point to a certain action and also to a previous action advocating or demanding the observed effect, without it being possible to demonstrate the link between the two. Here, where caution is the only guide, rashness has a way of pressing to the front. Thus it is far too often taken for granted that a piece of evidence demanding certain types of action was the cause, or at least the origin, of that action if that action can be shown to have taken place. "Ask and it shall be given unto you" is one text that simple historians seem to see readily fulfilled in their reconstruction of the past, and the prehistory of great movements—where the true answers are horribly complex—are peculiarly beset by this simplifying error. One historian can explicitly regard Erasmus' writings against monasticism as the real reason why monasteries were dissolved all over Europe in the early sixteenth century;[6] others adhere trustingly to the view that the many drastic changes in English government in the nineteenth century came about because Jeremy Bentham taught people to make them.[7] Few things are more difficult to prove than the effects of writings, especially writings of protest, upon the actual event, and in few things the historian—always tempted to overvalue the effect of rational persuasion, and professionally exposed to an excessive faith in the written word—shows greater readiness to ignore the warnings of experience and the caution taught him in his youth. The assessment of these materials of discussion involves him in allowing for and distinguishing between a variety of possibilities: direct cause-and-effect relationships, the creation of a general predisposition in favor of the action advocated, the coincidence of like-minded attitudes not derived from one another, and a total lack of any relationship at all. All are possible: there may be, and often will be, evidence to decide which applies.

This particular problem does not arise with the first group of records of discussion (those which embody activities of the agency active later), but these only raise other difficulties. Action is often preceded by some sort of study or investigation, and such investigations are occasions which do tend to leave evidence behind. The main pitfall here lies in the fact that the investigators appear to behave like historians: they appear to be concerned to disentangle the facts of a situation as fully and as impartially as may be. Thus, by appealing to a likeness, they can tempt the historian into treating them as equals, rather than as the producers of material still to be subjected to the historian's customary critical analysis. For a good example of this, let us look at the various types of investigating committees which have always been much used in England to consider problems and advise action, ever since the general enquiry into land tenure which produced *Domesday Book* in 1086. Medieval and early-modern commissions of enquiry (which did exist in very large numbers, mostly dealing with individual cases) have their own difficulties for the historian, among which the fact must rank high that as a rule only part of their evidential potential survives (perhaps only their report without the evidence on which it was based, or worst of all only the document appointing them). Sometimes we may have only a secondhand account of what was allegedly discovered and proposed, as with the reports on the state of the English monasteries produced by Thomas Cromwell's commissioners in 1535, apparently laid before Parliament but lost since and only known from the summaries provided by some chroniclers and a few extant letters. The cry went up, "Away with them!" we are told. Are we, then, to accept as a historically valid answer that the reading of reports, now gone, played a significant part in bringing about the Dissolution by directly moving the Parliament to promote or support the necessary bill? In this case, the inadequacy of the argument is obvious, and indeed, manifest incompleteness of the evidence alerts the least sensitive of historians; when, in addition, a very obvious bias can be suspected in the enquiry (as in the last example cited) he is more likely to be too skeptical than too trusting.

However, the opposite danger exists when the evidence survives complete; of this, an excellent example may be found in nineteenth-century England. This is a period exceptionally noisy with various enquiries and their reports. We possess the fact of appointment and names of members, the terms of reference, the record of investigation with witnesses' evidence, and the resultant conclusions of the investigators; on top of that, we shall often find subsequent and illuminating comment in the press or in Parliament, or elsewhere. On the face of it, no one could ask for a more thorough or more confidence-inspiring analysis of this or that problem—problems, moreover, which the historian needs to solve if he is to tell his story. Thus it is no wonder that a good deal of the history of the time, both social and political, has been written straight out of such evidence and with a ready trust in it. The whole conventional history of the effects of the early Industrial Revolution really stems from the reports of such investigations in the first half of the nineteenth century (especially as they seemed to confirm the more impressionist contemporary descriptions), and not at all from a detailed study of the facts behind the reports or ignored by the reports.[8]

In the process, historians have too often forgotten the first question they must ask of all evidence: why and by whom was this material produced? If they had done so, they would, in the first place, have discovered that they were faced by two quite different types of investigation— the royal commission and the parliamentary select committee. Royal commissions are usually composed of the noninvolved; very real attempts are made to create a balance of interests; they proceed by the legal methods established in the courts, have powers to examine on oath, and (as a rule) take a very long time. In consequence they actually provide one of the most satisfactorily impartial and accurate sources of information.[9] The select committee, on the other hand, is so composed as to reflect the balance of parties in the House of Commons and may be constructed by crusading individuals or pressure groups to suit themselves; it consists exclusively of members of the House, cannot examine on oath, and follows a procedure which one may charitably call flexible. Often enough it is set up to confirm a previous opinion or advance a set policy, and the tenor of its report can be entirely predictable. This is not to say that its work is altogether useless to the historian, though generally speaking it is the evidence printed in the appendixes rather than the conclusions and recommendations offered in the report which, rightly, have attracted attention. What should be obvious is that such materials require very different treatment from the outcome of royal commissions, that the purpose and manner of the enquiry necessitate stringent controls in the use of this evidence, the best that internal analysis, checking against establishable fact, and contextual criticism can do. At the same time, remembering that both types of enquiry not only yield information on particular issues but represent records of discussion preliminary to action, the committee reports, so obviously intended to prepare the ground for action, may be more revealing than the labors of those august and impartial and forgotten commissions.

Sometimes such records of investigation conceal technical problems which, when ignored, completely distort the historian's account. Thus historians wishing to understand the inward condition and general reputation of the medieval Church, for instance, naturally enough rely on the reports of ecclesiastical visitations. Here we have the leaders of the Church themselves looking at the parts of it and reporting on what they find without any thought of later generations: here, therefore, one would expect to discover a picture of the state of the Church which should help to explain attacks on it or its powers of resistance to attacks, and similar things. It is obviously possible that the visitors may have been biased or the institutions visited capable of hiding things, but such potential sources of distortion are readily allowed for. The real problems arise from the circumstances surrounding the production of this evidence, the technical structure of the ecclesiastical process of which visitations formed a part, and these have been commonly overlooked. The visitors recorded what they found and they issued injunctions which reflected the wrongs they thought needed remedy, but this did not cover the part of their work most striking to the historian interested in the state of the clergy. For a considerable part of their findings they acted as accusers, not as judges. Where a visitation found things manifestly amiss that were within the visitors' powers to amend (as the condition of a building or an open state of disharmony in a monastery), the report ends the matter by telling those involved to do better—to repair the chancel or behave like Christians. But where the visitors found punishable delicts—and this includes all the personal faults of the clergy alleged against them so often both in contemporary satire and historians' summaries—they could only record a charge which needed following up and proving in a court of law.

Thus just where the reports become most revealing for the answering of the standard questions they really tell only a very inconclusive story. One then needs to investigate whether the accused were subsequently convicted of the charge made, and quite apart from the extreme difficulty, in many cases, of finding the additional evidence, it is obvious (and always remembered in other similar cases where one knows of charges made but not proven) that many accusations may very well have been false. But historians considering the moral or intellectual standards of, say, the late-medieval clergy have very commonly accepted the allegations of a visitation as equal to the truth, and there cannot be much doubt that in consequence they have produced badly distorted descriptions which in turn have been used to form the very insecure foundation for general

analyses of the "causes" of the Reformation and similar
things.[10] Unfortunately, as so often, a better understanding
of the evidence here removes certainties and puts merely
question marks in their place, but that cannot be helped:
better an awareness of ignorance than confident error.
Much the same sort of error and consequences may be
illustrated by another sixteenth-century problem, that of
the enclosure of common lands. Here confident figures for
the area enclosed have been worked out and confident conclusions stated regarding their political significance, from
records of investigation which constituted only the first
stage in a process that required subsequent action and
proof in the courts.[11]

I have labored this at length because such serious mis-
interpretations occur all the time, in all forms of historical
study: what appears to be a safe contemporary analysis of
a situation is accepted as "true" historical evidence when a
real understanding of the material at once shows it not to
be so—or not necessarily to be so—and on the grounds of
that analysis, highly misleading political history gets written
which, since it usually has the support of some inclination
in historian and reader alike, soon becomes almost im-
movable orthodoxy. Any historian who has ever tried to
break down such ossified and sacred structures by pointing
out the insecurity of the foundations knows only too well
how hard the row is that he has chosen to hoe; and if in
the process he finds himself forced to question some
morally based view of the past—especially if he has to point
out that the alleged historical basis for the many entrenched "progressive" beliefs does not exist—he will be
lucky to escape with any reputation at all. Mankind prefers
its comfortable legends and expects the historian to lend
the appearance of rational soundness to them, nor is mankind to be blamed for this because the truth is often very
uncomfortable. But the historian deserves blame who, for

the sake of his own moral comfort, will ignore or, worse, attack the new truths which a skeptical investigation of the historical tradition produces. A generation or so ago, the errors needing and receiving attack were mostly of a conservative and complacent kind, and attacks on such errors enjoyed the benefit of the obvious sincerity and compassion which so often shines through the scientific work of the radical reformer. But the radical reformers have set up far more inaccurate legends than ever they demolished, and in attacking them one has, unhappily, to join issue with men whose hearts were all in the right place, no doubt, but who could tell a useful lie with less qualms than most because they were so sure of their own righteousness.

These are the problems of the battlefield, and it is after all a war in which no one needs to engage unless he wants to. But the situation underlines the need for stressing the obvious, and the points here made ought to be obvious. Of course, one should always know exactly what one's documents and records mean. But in the prehistory of political action, this specific not only has been too often ignored; it is in fact frequently very hard to observe. The best historians can perpetuate error, and they do so the more readily when they are trying to make intelligible the least palpable of past events. Among these the bases and origins of actions stand high. When all is said, the actual discussions which lead to decisions are, after all, rarely documented at all. At least before the nineteenth century, it is only very occasionally that one finds such points recorded, though now and again letters, memoranda, or even minutes of transactions may preserve part of the exchange of views and clashes of personalities from which action commonly results. Earlier history suffers from a lack of such evidence, not only because it always has less evidence but also because the further back one goes the less public government becomes; and where one encounters essentially single-person government, the discussion may often have taken place inside one man's mind. At times the historian may feel that he is always dealing with people like Oliver Cromwell who apparently decided upon his actions only after receiving personal instructions from God. At this point historical evidence is bound to end, and the historian has the choice of forgetting about the antecedents of action or venturing a speculative guess. The guess may be sensible or absurd—a point to be judged by contextual probability— but it always remains open to question and may on occasion be upset by new evidence. Letters or statements do come to light which at least cast doubts on long-held views about motive, intent, and initiative; alternatively, a rethinking of the context, on the basis of evidence not connected with these prehistories of action, may render the earlier prob- ability unlikely and substitute a new one for it.[12] Yet even when this sort of inner evidence exists, once in a while, it can remain difficult to know what to do with it. The dissolu- tion of the English monasteries has been used to illustrate the historian's difficulties more than once; let it serve once more. It has commonly been supposed that the dissolution represented Thomas Cromwell's particular policy and that therefore the manner in which it was brought about, (especially the use of an act of Parliament) may safely be ascribed to him.[13] Recently, however, an account has come to light according to which Cromwell wanted to proceed by piecemeal dissolution and was overruled in the Council by the opinion of those who advocated comprehensive action.[14] No one knows how the informant in this case came by the story, and the historian, presented with an interesting but completely unassessable piece of political history, hardly knows what to do with it.

The records of discussion (as I have termed them) are thus extremely complicated and difficult, which is to say that in the writing of political history the stages before

decisions are taken are usually the most problematical and
carry the greatest amount of uncertainty and controversy.[15]
The "why" in most cases remains forever disputable, which
is not to say that it should therefore be left out of account.
Of course, the historian is right to want to know and discover it. Moreover, answers so much more probable than
others that they come close to trustworthy certainty can
certainly be offered in many instances. The point is that the
facts attaching to historical evidence differentiate these
questions from those concerning the "that" (the event)
which are by comparison rendered relatively simple by the
evidence. Records of decision are of two kinds: those that
specifically document the occasion of decision-making and
those that embody and convey the decision made. The first
are mostly minutes of meetings or entries in daybooks—
notations of the actual event made at the time—though
entries found in later recollections of the words of a participant may sometimes be worth using. The second consist of
orders, issued mostly in letter form (which includes the
formalized writ). The first, however, also includes such
records as public announcements (inscriptions, proclamations, entries in official newspapers) all of which are alike
in pinpointing a usually debatable occurrence, the occasion
on which a certain decisive step was taken or on which it
was decided to do a certain thing. When this fact is recorded in isolation, the material has limited but absolutely
safe use: it cannot tell much, but that little it tells for certain, because one can say what was decided upon and
when.

True, dates can mislead; decisions can be announced
later or even earlier than in fact they became real, and
occasionally some are announced that have never been
taken at all. But these really are insignificant problems,
capable of simple solutions or unlikely to affect the story
seriously, compared with the fact that such statements of

decisions rarely exist in such isolated condition and are more commonly mingled with elements of the preceding and subsequent stages of development—with records of discussions and records of results. The minutes of governing bodies vary in this respect. The English Privy Council of the sixteenth century very rarely noted any part of the discussion, and its *Acts* are essentially a record of decisions; but consequences (what letters must be written or who is to be called up for what reason, for instance) inevitably make their appearance. The records of the modern Cabinet, on the other hand, like those of the Venetian Signory, include an abstract of the discussion. The historian must forever be aware of the peculiarities of the record before him: before he writes any real kind of political history, he must learn thoroughly what the material, by its nature, will tell him and what it will conceal. Merely reading it, however intelligently, is not enough.

By way of example, let us look at the materials of the English House of Commons. Before 1547 it produced records of neither discussion nor decision, but only a species of what I have called records of consequence in the documents embodying the statutes agreed to, to which one House of Parliament, of course, only contributed a part.[16] From 1547, a *Journal* of the House exists which began by being mainly a record of decisions (the various stages of the business done) but soon acquired a good deal of "discussion material" (debates) whose inclusion depended on the will or whim of the clerk. This mixed record endured till approximately 1660, after which date organization set in and the *Journal* became what it still is—a straight and complete record of decisions which tells nothing at all about the debates in the House. A proper record of these was a long time coming, and before the publication of a full transcript of debates (Hansard) was officially agreed upon round about 1900, the historian depends on various reports, some semiofficial and some avowedly private, whose reliability needs assessing. They range from the diaries of members to newspaper reports and include the seemingly official but in fact quite private precursors of Hansard; the one thing that unites them is their known failure to reproduce speeches either accurately or in full. Thus for this institution, the record of decisions is reasonably complete and very reliable for the last 400-odd years but nonexistent for the first 200 years of its life; the record of discussion is complete only for less than the last century but frequently available back to about 1570 in forms varying from the full to the very thin. The record problems are many and extend well beyond the existence of gaps. In using the *Journal,* for instance, the historian must always distinguish between its reliability as a record of decisions and its variability as a record of discussion.

However, the main body of evidence for political action consists of records of consequence, that is, of materials embodying the results of decisions. Indeed, decisions themselves are more commonly known from their results than from direct evidence, plentiful though that may be. This part of the political historian's material is too varied, complex, and unsystematic to be classified. It includes such things as orders or communications resulting from a political act, legislation, negotiations, records of police or court action, evidence about the movements of individuals or armies—the whole gamut of the political event insofar as it is preserved in documentary material rather than narrative. With it must be linked the last class, evidence of counteraction or reaction—response, protest, evasion. This last body of records appears in this light when seen from the point of view of the original action; looked at the other way, it in turn becomes a record of consequence, that is, of action taken as the result of a decision. Most of the material used by the political historian is of this kind, and the earlier stages of discussion, deliberation, and decision must often be inferred from it. There are dangers in this.

To take some examples. The historian of the Tudor Privy Council, looking at its surviving records, comes to realize that certain changes in composition and organization took place. He finds that before about 1530 the Council had a large and mixed membership of about fifty, but that after 1540 it consisted of nineteen men and that other earlier councilors, though still alive, are no longer members of the full body. From this he is led to infer that some time in the intervening ten years a decision was taken to alter the composition of the Council, but he has to base this conclusion (which is of some importance) on records of consequence (the material testifying to membership) because no record of the actual decision exists, and he therefore cannot assign an exact date to the event. This does not, however, remove the event from the category of knowable and known facts. On the other hand, one finds a resolution of August 10, 1540 appointing a clerk and a minutebook: here a record of decision pinpoints the event precisely. It would therefore seem that, while we can be sure of the second event, the first must always be based on conjecture, however persuasive. In point of fact, in this instance almost the reverse is true, a necessary warning to consider nothing as proven until it is—until the context of the evidence has been imaginatively considered. The record, elsewhere, contains sufficient indications that a clerk and minutebook (not now extant) existed before 1540, so that what happened on the recorded occasion amounted to a renewal or revival of an earlier arrangement, or perhaps only to a formal notice of existing practice. On the other hand, however uncertain the date of the Council's reorganization may be, the fact that it was reorganized within known limits of time is perfectly certain and proved beyond doubt by the newly invented distinction used in describing various classes of councilors. Thus the record of consequence, indirect though it may be, can be more reliable than the seemingly definite record of decision.

For an example of things working the other way, let us look at the Battle of Britain of 1940. The records of consequence testify to the assembling of invasion fleets and the purposeful stepping-up of air attacks. Allowing for some argument about the exact weight of all this, the evidence supports the notion that the Germans had decided to invade England, and this conclusion is backed up by a good many public statements of intent (themselves records of consequence). It therefore for a long time seemed safe to tell the story of 1940 on the assumption that after the fall of France Hitler meant to conquer Britain by invasion, attempted to do so, and was defeated. The opening of the archives, however, brought to light records of discussion and decision which cast doubt on this reconstruction and suggest that only a show of strength was intended, or that there was no firm agreement on the German side as to what should be done. The original view has not been destroyed, but it has been severely modified. The evidence of consequences proved to be too simple, too clear cut.

Thus the fact that most records available to the political historian are those of consequence and reaction must render him cautious, not only in assessing motive or cause but even in assembling the story of the event itself. Much of the time he argues from observable action back to a decision and a purpose and even an antecedent history. He is forced to ascribe deliberate intent and rational assessment, or at any rate some sort of previous action, to actors who have left no direct evidence of any such things. Common sense and common experience do indeed show that very often such extrapolation must be right: people do plan and decide their actions, and frequently something very like the intended action does come about. But common sense and common experience also show that some actions result from accident and others turn out very different from what was planned and decided. It is usually easier to assume that a given event can be explained rationally, but everyone knows that this need not be true. Historians react according to temperament. Some like to think that everything is the work of individuals operating purposefully; some prefer to believe that great oaks grow from little acorns, and that "big" events are the product of the trivial and accidental. The sensible historian will keep both possibilities in mind. But he should shun one way out of the dilemma, the explanation which removes the individual altogether and substitutes the operation of impersonal forces or the dialectic of artificial categories (class, ideal types, or even God and the Devil). It is legitimate to ascribe the French Revolution to the cumulative grievances of certain identifiable groups of people and the failure of other people, caught up in the system, to provide remedies; and it is possible, though naive, to ascribe it to Necker or Mirabeau or a temporary shortage of bread. What is not in order is the explanation which falls back on the rise of the bourgeoisie, the alienation of the professional classes, or the inevitable consequences of the Enlightenment. These sort of phrases need enlargement in terms of human participation and activity.

The type of record available thus decides on the one hand the forms of story and explanation, and on the other the degree of reliability in either. Where all four categories exist the political historian can re-create the event with a very high degree of completeness and truthfulness. Where, as is much more common especially for periods thinly documented, everything has to be developed (inferred) from the facts of action only (and these sometimes pretty fragmentary too), the reconstruction has to rely on degrees of probability. Political historians are so used to discovering deliberation and decision from consequences that even to themselves they often blur the important differences; and they should therefore be more consciously aware of the type of record available to them. This might, on the one hand, prevent overconfident ascriptions of intent or identifications of main actors when no direct evidence exists. To say that Jefferson did this or Bismarck did that, without further argument, should be reserved for the occasions on which records of decision exist, and while for these two statesmen they often do, the point becomes much more problematical if one has to deal with Mark Antony or Frederick Barbarossa. In such cases—the vast majority—the statement that a man did something or was responsible for something has to be argued through in terms of inferential evidence and probability. On the other hand, attention to the difference should also prevent the writing-off of proper evidence. Thus A. J. P. Taylor, by looking at records of consequence, could construct a reasonably convincing argument that Hitler did not intend war in 1939, or perhaps ever; as always, this type of record made possible more than one inference with respect to intent and decision. But Mr. Taylor also, in the process, disallowed valid and strong evidence of intent and decision which does exist, largely by treating it as though it were like evidence of consequences and therefore open to the same sort of skepticism. The differences arise from the fact that all evidence provides certainty for its own immediate content-matter but speculation concerning the before and after and around; where intent is in question, evidence of decision is firm, evidence of consequences is adjustable.[17]

One other point about the records of political history is worth noting. In the main they are letters of one kind and another, though, of course, other kinds of documents also occur. But letters form the bigger part of them. This is not true for all historians; indeed, for most types of historical

writing letters, whether official or private, provide a comple-
ment to the evidence, not its main structure. In political
history they compose the bulk of the records of consequence, though they are less dominant among those of
discussion or decision; but since, as has been said, records
of consequence themselves predominate, letters assume a
disproportionate importance.[18] This has some unexpected
consequences. Letters are the most general, least formal,
of all records, and they are essentially nonsystematic. This
means, on the one hand, that they are the most human of
documents, reveal individual minds and personalities, and
make possible an analysis of motives, purposes, feelings,
and interactions. Much of the attraction of political history
flows from this. But nonsystematic evidence is evidence
full of unpredictable and uncomfortable gaps. Unlike series
and unlike impersonal records, it resists quantification and
continuous ordering, so that political history has more
uncertainties, inferences, and breaks not to be filled in by
reasonable extrapolation from either end than is true, for
instance, of economic history; and it has far more genuine
conjecture than the history of ideas.

Moreover, the informality of letters raises a problem
rarely mentioned and apparently little known. Letters are
not technical in the sense in which financial accounts or
the records of law courts are technical; they have little
common form by which to judge their place, purpose, and
(sometimes) date; and they seem straightforward. The
historian working with formal and technical records has to
understand their forms and technicalities; in the process he
acquires an assurance in handling materials which enables
him to judge the penumbra of meanings accurately. Letters
do not teach this, and a historian who uses only, or almost
only, documents of this type lacks the technical assurance
of his colleague. History written out of letters only is exceptionally restricted in its technical competence—which is

one reason why traditional diplomatic history, built up mainly out of despatches, can be so unsatisfactory and so unreal. It may seem odd to assert that the most personal and individual type of document should produce a specially unreal type of history, and the unfortunate effect need not, of course, follow; but often it does. When it does, I think that apart from failure of imagination on the historian's part the main reason lies in the peculiarly untechnical character of letter evidence. It neither strains the professional understanding of the historian (everyone supposedly can understand letters) nor thereby develops the muscles of his analytical reason. Again, once the danger is recognized it can be overcome; even letters contain some technicalities and impersonal problems, and evidence of other types can usually be found to be relevant and necessary. But if people rightly complain that so much political history seems intellectually unsatisfying, they should realize that this has to do not so much with the questions asked or the competence of the historian, but with the nature of his material which can be intellectually so much less demanding than most.

One obvious and easy remedy lies in the fact that political history, as has already been said, involves an understanding of the structure and development of the system whose political career is being investigated. The materials of constitutional and administrative history are, by and large, very different from those of political history narrowly conceived. Here one deals with institutions—a working machine which must be understood from its products and processes—and with the principles which fit them together into a system of government. These things must be discovered from their own stated rules, from formal comment, from the technicalities of actual operations, and now and again from outside description. Since the political historian needs to understand the instruments by means of which policy is conducted, he must become familiar with these materials, too. He will find them to be essentially analytical rather than narrative, but he will also find a good deal of overlap with his more familiar sources. The records of cabinets, departments, agencies of finance, and courts of law consist of the deposit of such matters as are there administered. In the first place they are likely to contain a good deal of the material which has been described as records of discussion and decision for political history. This is obvious for the cabinet type of record, the product of the policy-making sector of government. But departments, too, contribute to this. However, the main part of these records does not fit into the categories delineated in this chapter. They testify to action in, rather than action by, these institutions (though the latter is not entirely absent nor always distinguishable from the former), and their precise character depends on their technical competence, on the area of government covered.

Thus a financial department keeps records which result from its business in accounting for the income and expenditure of government money: receipts and issues, audits, the securing of outstanding items. A court of law keeps records of the litigation there conducted. A chancery preserves materials relating to secretarial activity and government patronage (appointments to office, and so forth). At all times these documents are technical. That is to say, they can be understood only if the administrative processes producing them are understood; they are formal, and their common form must be learned; they are impersonal and hardly ever reflect the personal or individual existences of the people who produced or handled them. Thus they require very different treatment by the historian from the materials of political history proper, which has the technical advantage that it gives him an additional dimension to his training and equipment. Much political history has been written in ignorance of such matters and materials, and it is very much the worse for it. Not only does this ignorance entail the omitting of important questions and the misunderstanding of many more, but it produces an essentially superficial and unquestioning mind. Many discussions, for instance, of English parliamentary history, especially since the Middle Ages, are marred by the historian's ignorance of the technical materials and rules governing the affairs of the Parliament. People solemnly search for the motives behind an action when all the time what was done resulted only from the established methods of doing business there, indicated no choice or policy on anybody's part, and cannot be analyzed in these "political" terms at all.[19] Ignorance of the financial techniques of different ages is so commonplace that books getting the facts of income and expenditure wrong are really rather more common than those that get them right. And ignorance of law and legal process is probably the besetting endemic disease of political historians who yet are frequently forced to deal with the consequences of legal action. Before the middle of the seventeenth century at any rate, a great deal of the political activity of European governments and individual people got deposited in legal records which simply cannot be understood aright without an effort of learning.

The effects of this brand of ignorance have probably been worst in social history, as in the orthodoxy established by Tawney's work on sixteenth-century agrarian society which has already been mentioned,[20] but the political historian has been very far from immune, especially as his interpretation of events is often determined by the analysis of the economic and social historian. Error mediated at one remove is the harder to detect. To follow up the last example: the history of Tudor popular unrest and its effects has been badly distorted by historians of the economy who misunderstood the law and therefore also the economy itself, with the result that the partisan allegations of the day came to be treated as historical truths. Or again, the violent politics of Henry VIII's reign have been sadly misdescribed by some historians who had no conception of the law and legal process which bound government even in matters of treason and sedition. One side among the participants in some very large debates, and, commonly, the side which least understood the facts behind the obvious troubles of its day, has been endowed with the sole possession of righteousness. This happens all the time, and much rewriting of history, often resented by those who in their youth have been instructed in the hoary errors, consists simply of asking whether the *structure* of the historical scene really supports the story as told.

The correct understanding of these issues on the edge of the purely political depends on a correct understanding of the relevant records, and the political historian, intent on telling the story of a society in political action, really cannot afford to ignore any documentary material surviving for his time. Not all of it will by any means be relevant for him, but a great deal is ignored at peril. It is here that the bare outline provided by narrative sources finds its vast corrective and addition: the true and full story depends on documentary records, and they must be the historian's main study. But even narratives and documents do not exhaust the evidence available to him—or, by another token, the evidence it behoves him to consider. There is, lastly, what one may call evidence of reflection and comment. By this I mean the writings, usually contemporary or nearly so, which consider the facts of political organization and action and express views on them. This material may be summed up as book learning, and it ranges from the descriptive through the analytical to the philosophical. There are books (whether printed or not) which give an account of an institution; there are books or newspaper editorials (to be distinguished from the reporting of events) which comment favorably or adversely on something done; there are the works of political philosophers from Plato to Marcuse. All these—and the categories include much that has been barely hinted at in this brief description—are relevant to the political historian, but in a special way. It is not his task to write the history of ideas, but it is his task to understand the ideas and feelings which contributed to political action or reaction or comprehension. Thus, to him this large area of historical materials is secondary but still essential, to be known and incorporated into the account of political events and their circumstances, but to be controlled by the primary record and treated with the critical instruments designed to discover events, not opinions or philosophical positions.

The common error here, as a matter of fact, has been to treat the critical or philosophical accounts as equal in value and purpose to narratives—to produce a thin sort of synthesis out of the two and use the main evidence (records) merely to fill in or illustrate. From the far too many examples that jump to the mind—especially the mind of a historian working in the era of the Reformation—a striking one may be selected. The history of the violent political conflicts of the seventeenth century in England was for long written under the authoritative weight of one seventeenth-century party's views, producing a purely whig account. The use of contemporary pamphlets only reinforced this established and integrated interpretation because most pamphlets came from the parliamentary, puritan, or whig side, while those that did not were overlooked in the mass by eyes conditioned to see one side only. Even historians who did try to discover the other point of view confined their materials to royalist statements of policy and royalist pamphleteers. Not even letters, the obvious record material to be used, received any systematic or exhaustive treatment, and the bulk of the available records—technical, difficult, seemingly remote—was altogether ignored. Thus, for instance, an assessment of Charles I's personal rule either condemned it on the strength of contemporary condemnations and a few leading cases, or praised it on the strength of certain noble intentions expressed by men on the king's side; what actually happened, what was actually done, what in fact all this turmoil meant, remained hidden in voluminous, entirely accessible, but rather more difficult records.[21] The prehistory of the American Revolution for long received much the same treatment, nor is it clear that even today the effects of the English trade system or of the taxes imposed on the colonies are not more commonly described from the complaints of contemporaries than from a study of the fiscal records. Any area of political history readily provides examples of the disasters which befall when of the three main categories of materials available to him the historian prefers the easier (narratives and comments) and shies away from the documentary record which should be his chief reliance.

Recognition of this fact can, in turn, have its own dangers. Namier's insistence that eighteenth-century parliamentary affairs must be analyzed from the record, and his unfortunate concentration only on the records explaining the positions and personalities of elected members, have certainly obscured far too much and turned too many of his less able followers against all other forms of evidence. Thus they quite improperly neglect not only the older narratives (which can sometimes teach them things at which they laboriously arrive themselves)[22] but especially the literature of comment in which the ideas behind action and the purposes of politics are mainly deposited. Indeed, in their love affair with the records they have even forgotten that the institution they profess to study itself left records, an extraordinary lapse.[23]

In truth, the political historian cannot afford to neglect any of the materials proper to his study, and nearly all historical materials are. Narratives give him the first ordering of the story; records enable him to tell it properly, in truthful detail and in correction of error; comment assists in explaining action and amplifying its implications. Of all three, the records are his master because they are most completely divorced from the storytelling purpose that inspires him and therefore contribute least to the natural biases in himself which his study of evidence is designed to correct. Between them, these three types do not exhaust the materials of history in general, but they do form an inordinately large part of it. Political history is written because it can be written. It is, however, hard to write well because its materials are so exceptionally massive, so very varied, and demand such manifold abilities, insights, and skills from the historian. And the major difficulty hidden in the evidence should also by now have become plain. It usually makes possible the piecing together of what happened, and that in itself is a great virtue. However, the political historian wants to explain his story and make sense of it—to show why things happened and why people did this or that. Here his materials give him much less help because the historical record always leaves it to the historian to discover the causes of action and motives of men. What is more, the whole question of how, or even whether, one can explain history—the question of causation—is fraught with difficulties. What does the political historian mean when he *explains* the course of events?

NOTES

1. This is not to deny that all historians should read one another. The present spate of professional historiography, so welcome in most respects, suffers too often from failure to note what has already been done. The results are duplication of effort and—much worse—failure to comprehend problems already clarified elsewhere. A learned work whose footnotes include few or no references to other learned works displays at best remediable ignorance, at worst envy and a false desire to seem original.

2. Cf. the difficulty experienced in writing a convincing story of eighteenth-century politics ever since Namier introduced the disorder of reality into what had been a well-fixed and ordered arrangement based on fundamental misunderstandings.

3. The memoirs of the French revolutionary era come to mind as an example of what can be done; those of World War II as an example of what needs doing. Some modern editions, especially of letters and especially those produced so lavishly in the United States, confuse efficient editing with painful pedantry, and the massive notes added to the Yale edition of Thomas More's *Utopia* (ed. J. H. Hexter and E. Surtz, 1965) look a great deal more complete and important than they are.

4. I am qualified to speak only of the editing of English historical materials which, for postmedieval history, leaves a good deal to be desired. Editors omit what they are pleased to consider insignificant documents in a chain of events (Isabel M. Calder, ed., *Activities of the Puritan Faction of the Church of England 1625–1633* [London, 1957]: this leaves out writs to which the documents printed are the response); they remove formulae which alone establish the precise character of the material on the grounds that common-form phrases are superfluous (P. Hughes and J. F. Larkin, eds., *Tudor Royal Proclamations* [3 vols., New Haven, 1964, 1969]); instead of listing and systematically describing the manuscripts edited, they bury them uselessly inside a "literary" preface (Elizabeth R. Foster, ed., *Proceedings in Parliament 1610* [New Haven, 1966]). Of course there are many valuable things about such editions—including the three here cited—but this makes the needless inefficiencies only worse. There are standard practices in use among the editors of ancient and medieval materials of which those of more recent documents do not seem to have heard.

5. Cf. Gordon Leff, *History and Social Theory* (London, 1969), p. 21.

6. H. A. Enno van Gelder, *The Two Reformations in the 16th Century* (The Hague, 1961), p. 150.

7. See the controversy between Oliver MacDonagh and Henry Parris in *Hist. Journal* 1 (1958): 55ff., and 3 (1960): 1ff.

8. Some of the most influential work in this area was done by

J. L. and Barbara Hammond in their studies of the early industrial working classes. Their methods of study, certain to produce support for foregone conclusions, are analyzed by W. H. Hutt, "The Factory System of the Early Nineteenth Century," in *Capitalism and the Historian*, ed. F. Hayek (London, 1954), p. 16off.

9. Cf. Charles J. Hauser, *Guide to Decision: The Royal Commission* (Totowa, N. J., 1965).

10. For a description of the materials, cf. *An Episcopal Court Book for the Diocese of Lincoln 1514–1520*, ed. M. Bowker, Lincoln Record Society 61 (Lincoln, 1967): esp. pp. xi–xii.

11. E. Kerridge, "The Returns of the Inquisition of Depopulation," *English Historical Review* 70 (1955): 212–228.

12. Cf., e.g., my attempt to reconsider the parts played by Henry VIII and Thomas Cromwell in the English Reformation, on the basis of a revised view of the reign as a whole: "King or Minister?" *History* (1954), p. 216ff.

13. E.g., G. R. Elton, *England under the Tudors* (London, 1955), p. 144; D. Knowles, *The Religious Orders in England* (Cambridge, 1959), 3:291.

14. *The Papers of George Wyatt, Esquire*, ed. D. M. Loades (Camden, 4th Series, vol. 5; London, 1968), p. 159.

15. In consequence, some historians seem to wish to discard the study of cause, motive, and antecedent (below, p. 120).

16. I.e., the so-called Original Acts, the actual documents passing through Parliament, which are extant (with gaps) from 1497, and the enrollments of acts in the Statute Roll (which ceases in 1482) and the Roll of the Parliament which really record much more properly the affairs of the Lords. Cf. G. R. Elton, *The Sources of History: England 1200–1640* (London, 1969), p. 83ff.

17. I know that what people say they mean or meant to do may hide other real intentions, contain misleading rationalizations, or be dressed up to make them look more far-sighted than they were. To say that records of intent are firm is not to say that they do not require critical assessment, only that assessment is governed by the nature of the record and must not destroy, however much it may reconstitute, the fact of intent.

18. For the periods devoid of letter evidence, political history is therefore mainly dependent on narrative sources, a fact well known to ancient historians and medievalists. But note the enormous difference made to the precision and detail of the story by such a survival as Cicero's correspondence.

19. For a good example see the errors originated by the conviction that the different ways in which papers were laid before Parliament reflected political purposes, when all the time only the technicalities and conventions of debate and printing were at work. Cf. the article by Sheila Lambert, "A Century of Diplomatic Blue Books," *Hist. Journal* 10 (1967): 125ff.

20. Note 25, ch. 1.

21. Cf. the difference made to a part of history by the serious research embodied in Hugh Kearney's *Strafford in Ireland* (Man-

chester, 1959) and Aidan Clarke's *The Old English in Ireland 1625–1642* (London, 1966). The main story of government in England still awaits its historian.

22. H. Butterfield, *George III and the Historians* (London, 1957).
23. Above, p. 35.

CHAPTER 4

Explanation and Cause

In making sense of the past, the historian not only tries to discover what happened— and all that those two brief words involve —but also how the things that happened were linked one with another: their meaningful relationship. This activity may range from the minute to the macrocosmic: from understanding why someone was somewhere on a given day, through "the causes of the French Revolution," to the "patterns of world history" allegedly discoverable in retrospect. In essence, however, the activity is always the same: the bringing together of disparate events and disconnected individuals in an intelligible relationship which explains their coexistence in the historian's mind and thinking. In practice, the commonest, though not the only one, of these relationships has been that of cause and effect, a relationship defined (though the terms may well be implicit and silent) by the question "why" and the answer "because." This is the essentially rational relationship. It rests on the assumption that all the aspects of an event (facts as well as values, existence as well as import) can be perfectly ex-

plained (derived) from its antecedents, and it is obviously
attractive to the historian who with his chronological
method is naturally inclined to believe in the effect of
antecedents upon subsequents. To him, sequence in time
must mean more than mere sequence: though he will do
well to remember that causal relationships are not the only
ones possible, he necessarily seeks in the past not a nar-
ratively strung agglomeration of particles but an explanatory story of cause and effect. In addition, since he deals
with people, he naturally supposes that he can at least
make an effort to discover why people did things: he is
driven to analyze motives. Once the historian has gone past
the stage of mere discovery, cause and motive form his primary tools of analysis and organization; they are his paramount means for articulating the past and giving meaning
to it.

Both concepts have however been much attacked. The
literature on historical causality is voluminous and unending.[1]* It is full of high ingenuity and speaks well for philosophers' ability to argue logically about abstractions from
reality. For the most striking thing about it is its apparent
ignorance of what actually happens when a historian investigates the past and attempts to explain it. This stricture
applies most strongly to the rigorous logicians, but unhappily it has much truth also for those philosophers who
have made an effort to appreciate some of the peculiarities
of historical research. The fact comes out most obviously
in the persistent failure to choose sound examples with
which to illustrate the case. In all the discussion I have
read about historical explanation, I do not remember one
single citation from a historical monograph: none, that is,
from that category of historical work which is really concerned with establishing and explaining a piece of historical reconstruction. All the examples come either from
general works which are bound to take much of their con-

* Notes for this chapter begin on p. 152.

tent at secondhand, or (fortunately more rarely) from the higher-flown think-pieces about the meaning of history to which some historians are prone.

The former embody pared-down and commonly borrowed versions of the genuine and self-arrived explanation, in itself a proper and necessary thing in surveys and text-books, but no more than a contracted and often abstracted simplification of the real explanation offered in original work. By some accident, the philosophers do not, moreover, seem to choose the best books and writers, either. Sadly enough, the historians' friends among philosophers are particularly prone to these errors of judgment. Thus Dray uses a particularly inane statement from a particularly unimpressive historian, Ramsay Muir,[2] and Donagan re-sorts to the most general, most derived, and least important book of that prolific writer, J. A. Williamson.[3] In such cases, the "explanations" offered represent neither learning nor thought. One must also be struck by the frequency with which examples are chosen from ancient history, a testimony to philosophers' classical education but not to their acquaintance with history. When Donagan uses the murder of Caesar and sparing of Antony in order to discuss the problems of corroboration and *a priori* psychology in the discovery of motive, he never seems to realize that he has vitiated the argument by pinning it to an instance in which dearth of evidence makes any form of verification or denial a merely mental exercise.[4] Similarly, Gardiner distorts his argument about motive by using Caesar's cross-ing of the Rubicon: there are many people in history for whose motives more, and more varied, evidence survives than for Caesar's.[5]

The second area of choice, the think-pieces, yield those gnomic or universalist pronouncements which it is the task of serious historical analysis to test; most of them (to be moderate) fail the test and should hardly, therefore,

be cited as cases of historical explanation. Thus Charles
Frankel, who rightly regards interpretation in history as a
form of explanation, cites four of them: from the Communist Manifesto, Arnold Toynbee, H. A. L. Fisher, and
G. M. Young.[6] They are worth a look. The first reads thus:
"The history of all hitherto existing society is the history of
class struggles." This is an explanation, but it happens to be
empirically false.[7] As for the second—"Civilizations are
nothing but . . . efforts to move on from . . . the accom-
plished fact of Human Nature to another nature, super-
human or divine, which is the unattained goal of human
endeavours"—it is certainly untestable and would in fact
appear to be quite meaningless. The third is Fisher's famous
assertion that history can yield no generalizations but is the
play of the contingent and unforeseen; this is not, it seems
to me, an interpretation or explanation at all, but a method-
ology of explanation. The last ("the function of the nineteenth century was to disengage the disinterested intelligence, to release it from the entanglements of party and
sect—one might almost add of sex—and to set it operating
over the whole range of human life and circumstance") is
rather pretentious, rather empty, and in part demonstrable
nonsense; and the historian who commits the anthropo-
morphic error of endowing a period of time with an active
function can hardly be said to have offered an explanation
of history.

Even when the choice of examples is more considered
and shows a desire to come a little more up-to-date, it
comes to grief by its readiness to treat as useful cases of
historical explanation instances which historical research
has had little difficulty in discarding. Thus Donagan uses
Trevor-Roper's thesis concerning a rising and a falling
gentry in seventeenth-century England,[8] even though it
soon became apparent that an explanation which failed to
fit with the majority of the facts it was supposed to explain

can at best be a temporary hypothesis. I realize, of course, that from the point of view of the philosophical question the accuracy or penetration or comprehensiveness of the explanation are not particularly relevant, but I cannot help thinking that an argument which rests for preference on simplistic or unsupportable or rash examples of the matter under discussion is not coming to grips with the real problem at all.

The inadequacies of these methods are shown up very plainly in the thirteen examples which Gardiner lists in order to exemplify types of historical explanation.[9] He takes four from very general histories incorporating historical thinking at secondhand, two from Seignobos, and two from Trevelyan, both capable synthesizers but hardly analytical historians of any quality. Three come from textbook histories covering shorter periods: one again from the inevitable Trevelyan, one from Croce (not exactly at his best here),[10] and one from Stenton, the first really considerable historian using his own researches to appear here. There are two citations from popular biographies by Veronica Wedgwood and Bainville, one from Pirenne's brilliant and provocative book which deliberately dealt in unestablished sweeping generalizations, one from an undisguised piece of ideological propaganda unfettered by the principles of precise historiography (by Plekhanov), and one from a piece of undisguised ideological propaganda which tries to abide by these principles (Tawney). The tally is made up with a quotation from Leonard Woolf whom no one has ever supposed to be a historian. Now, of course, Gardiner's concern is with the fact that all these quotations embody one form or another of historical explanation, which they do. But his choice of authors and works necessarily biases and distorts the discussion. These are all compressed and quite insufficient statements, some of them remarkably jejune and some of them so wide as to offer no real explanation at all; some beg the question; some assert connections which no one can prove; not one can be considered profound or historically revealing, however useful they may be for logical classification. It is not too much to say that all philosophical analyses of cause, explanation, and interpretation in history have adopted the most unsophisticated view of the phenomenon investigated. The need to simplify in order to analyze may lie behind this refusal to study the real subject which it is pretended is being studied, but in the result it is plain that to tackle the philosophy of history thus from outside produces interesting but irrelevant discussion—irrelevant because the real problems of historical explanation are never touched. It has, of course, to be admitted that intimate acquaintance with the work of producing history is likely to remove all desire to philosophize about it.

More astonishing is the occasional inability of philosophers to maintain their own skills in working order the minute they approach historical statements. Thus Dray, quoting Ramsay Muir's remark about the later eighteenth century in England ("It was not merely an economic change that was thus beginning; it was a social revolution") asserts that here we have an explanation in answer to the question "what?" But even a cursory look at the statement shows that it is neither an explanation nor even a description in lieu of an explanation, but rather an emotional assertion without any precise value, intended to classify, it is true, but quite failing to do so. Unless we have an explanation of what Muir means by a social revolution and can in the end accept his explanation, and unless we are told just what the supposed contradiction is alleged to mean, we cannot derive any meaning, expository or explanatory, from the statement. Muir did not think that he was here explaining at all; he was using a phrase he had not thought through in order to end a paragraph.

This shows the danger of seeking examples in the wrong places, but it also shows the danger of treating quotations from historians as ready-made bricks in a wall, instead of first analyzing them to discover whether in themselves they have any use in the argument. There is a splendid case of this in the debate between Morton White and Patrick Gardiner over what constitutes a historical explanation as distinct from one proper to some other "intellectual discipline."[11] Leaving aside a philosophical argument which is wrong from the start because it arises from an attempt to divide up human knowledge not only according to the questions asked and the methods of enquiry employed but also by the areas of experience from which proof may be obtained, let us look at the bit of history they use. Gardiner, typically, produces a citation from that repository of bogus explanations (facile and often meaningless generalizations plus artificial discoveries of "influence"), G. M. Trevelyan's *English Social History*, to the effect that the hospitals founded in the 125 years after 1700 "were the outcome of individual initiative and coordinated voluntary effort and subscription." He and White then argue the peculiarly empty issue whether this explanation contains historical or sociological terms, or what. Neither of them asks whether it is an explanation with meaning, or what profitable depth of explanation it may offer. What Trevelyan was saying was in fact verbally wrong: the hospitals were not "the outcome" of the activities alleged, though these activities may have contributed to the fact that ultimately there were hospitals. So, of course, did need, the recognition that disease might perhaps be controlled in this way, the activities of builders and bricklayers, and other "factors." Unfortunately, Trevelyan singled out two that should have alerted the logician in our warring philosophers: he is saying that hospitals were built by some people because some people wanted to build hospitals. His explanation is a tautology which acquires meaning only when one restores what he left out: when one adds (which he *may* tacitly have understood) that they were not built by state action or compulsory taxation. It is the tautology of the statement that one would expect to strike the philosopher, the essential failure of this explanation to be an explanation. But neither philosopher remarks on it.

However, disappointing though much of this ardent discussion turns out to be, not all the arguments about historical explanation are so badly affected by the inexperience of the participants in the actual work of historical research, and even when they are they raise genuine problems which the working historian would do well to ponder now and again. This is the more desirable because, at a lower level of discussion, the whole idea of causation has come under attack for reasons connected with the difficulty of establishing independent or objective criteria for judging between one alleged cause and another. On the one hand, it seems quite often to be held that the multiplicity of past events prevents any precise definition of causality and therefore makes all historical explanations merely subjective; on the other, that the search for causes leads to a determinism which elevates the explanations most satisfactory to the inquirer's predilections to the status of a supposedly scientific demonstration. Subsidiary to this, one can find it argued that the historian has no way of discovering human motives: they do not belong to his province. Whether, with some philosophers, one reserves the search for motive to abstract ethics, or, with the psychologists, stresses the obvious fact that ostensible motive may hide a reality not provable from the historical record, one deprives the historian of the power to say convincingly that a man did this or that for this or that reason. The argument against cause and motive in history—even Gordon Leff's argument against treating causality as the main relationship between historical events[12]—can lead too readily to the removal of man from history.

The doubts cast upon the use of cause and motive in the analysis of the past have predictably led to some remarkable confusions, exemplified, for instance, in Geoffrey Barraclough's lecture on "History and the Common Man."[13] Attacking the alleged "wrong turning" taken by the writing of history in the nineteenth century, Barraclough wishes to turn historians from the search for causes and motives to a search for "facts." This harmless, though pointless, specific, which says no more than that we have still a lot of history to learn and more to rethink, conflicts strikingly with his other preference for "wide, systematic interpretations which, ultimately, are the justification of [historians'] work." How one is to achieve the second by practicing the first is not at all clear, and how "patterns of the past" significant for present and future understanding may be developed with no search for antecedent causes or even the much despised "origins" must remain totally obscure. Barraclough supposes that "if one-tenth of the energy which has gone into trying to apportion responsibility for the outbreak of war in 1914 had been devoted to studying its consequences, we might be further forward," and with this he thinks he has shown up the search for causes as the time-wasting enterprise he holds it to be. But what he has done is to switch from the causes of the war to the war as a cause—and to the search for the causes of a later stage of development. That is, in part he has not abandoned the search for causes at all, and in part he has redefined it by assuming in something the presence of a cause. For enquiry he has substituted assertion, not the most obvious of gains.

The fact is that no historian, trying to render intelligible a sequence and amalgam of events, can manage without establishing frequent causal relationships, or therefore do without some understanding of what causality may mean in history, if he is to get beyond the most primitive kind of chronicling. The choice he has does not lie between seeking causes and forgetting about them, but only between knowing the cause beforehand—as in such a scheme as Toynbee's in which a given stage in a civilization's "life" leads inevitably to another given stage—and empirically discovering it as best he may. And since to him (history being the record of men's actions) what men do or intend influences events, he is also bound to search for motives, if he is to get beyond a mere insertion of human beings into an otherwise impersonal and a-human story. The result, therefore, of the philosophical, psychological, and to some extent historiographical doubts cast upon the concept of cause has been not enlightenment but bewilderment.

Some historians help themselves by a purely verbal trick: they refuse to use the word cause and substitute the word factor whenever their predecessors, in their positivist way, would have crudely said cause.[14] Though this practice reflects a proper recognition of complexity to which I shall return, it is too often merely a device born of embarrassment and intrudes a misused cant term designed to ease the burden of intellectual decisions. Others again employ an alternative sleight of hand: causes of a particular kind make way for forces, with the result that events are conceived of as being directed by transcendent rather than specific circumstances and causality becomes determinism, without the unhappy word "cause" having to be used. This would seem to be the sort of explanatory pattern-making that Barraclough had in mind. Why the device should be supposed to solve the problem is a mystery. A cause is no less a cause for being big and woolly: the spirit of the times, national characteristics, human nature, the forces of the market, the class struggle, for that matter God, are all of the nature of causes when they are being used to give meaning to a historical situation or development, even if they excel by being imprecise, impressionistic, predetermined, or merely evasive, where the conventional search for causes looks for the particular and describable connection.[15] Perhaps the commonest evasion of straight causality in history is that which takes caution to the point of total obscurity: so aware are some historians of the complexity of problems and the difficulties posed by the whole notion that one thing may cause another that they prefer to assemble collections of often contradictory "elements" which may explain something or other, but themselves refuse to construct the explanation.

The only successful surrender to the supposed impropriety of the search for causes has been achieved at the cost of abandoning the study of history altogether and turning instead to the study of historians. If cause has no meaning in history, it is surely best to suppose that history itself has no meaning except in the mind of him who writes it, and in that case it is desirable to study him—his purposes and motives and operations—rather than what he supposed was an objective truth discovered by him. Here the flight from causality links hands with the other relativist interpretations of historians' labors—the doubts about objectivity, the existence of historical truth, and the distortions imposed by the need to select from an already selected part of the past's experience—to force a retreat away from the task altogether. The idealist tenets of Croce and Collingwood, who argued that history is what happens in historians' minds (the present reconstruction of the past), lead directly to this error.[16]

It is the political historian who must most obviously face the question whether he is entitled to speak in terms of cause and motive. Other forms of historical enquiry are less directly affected if these concepts lose validity. Economic and social history can more justifiably reduce the

difficult multiple causes, with their hidden content of subjective choice, to the generalized conditions, sometimes derived from theory rather than empirically from the
evidence, within which their subject matter moves. The
history of ideas will, in fact, do well to abandon one major
by-product of the passion for causes, the conviction that it
needs to study "influences"; here the attack on crude causality is doing nothing but good.[17] The history of art similarly hardly needs causes and motives; in studying the
products and placing them in the historical, social, and
intellectual context it rarely needs to ask why men produced them. None of these branches of historical study
will, or should, abandon altogether the reasonable enquiry
into origin and consequence—the chain of causality—but
it is not central for them. It is central for the political
historian whose primary task is the delineation of mankind
in political action: striving for power, exercising power,
losing power, creating or destroying the instruments and
embodiments of power. Here it is not only inescapable that
one should want to know why people did all these things
in given circumstances, but an understanding of this "why"
turns out to be the essence—in a way, the whole—of this
kind of history. Description without intelligibility, listing
without causal connections, neither demonstrate nor create
the sort of interest which one may fairly demand from any
intellectual enterprise. A word is therefore necessary in the
present discussion about the historian's understanding of
the term cause and about the problem of explanation in
history.

This discussion is rendered the more desirable by the
weaknesses of the philosophical discussion which has been
briefly analyzed. Apart from not quite understanding what
it is that the historian does, the philosophers have usually
been led astray by false analogies with the true claims of
the natural sciences to be searching for general laws, and

by the false claims of the social sciences to do the same. And even those philosophers, like Dray and Danto, who display a better understanding of the problem they discuss, arrive at unsatisfactory (truth to tell, rather imprecise and even muddled) conclusions because they do not succeed in grasping the actual processes of historical investigation and reconstruction. As we shall see, the intellectual conditioning of the logician is exactly opposed to that of the historian, so that the historian cannot really understand what the philosopher tells him about his *modus operandi*, while the philosopher, contemplating what the historian claims to be doing, feels either contempt or despair. More particularly, philosophers rightly proceed by a clarification of problems: that is, they reduce them to manageable proportions by eliminating the inessential and identifying the essential. The historian, on the other hand, never, or hardly ever, and never when anything like a real issue is at hand, deals in single or even few causes; his characteristic mode of procedure involves complicating every problem by making additions of more essentials to those first identified. Yet all the discussions of historical explanation that I have seen at heart assume single-cause situations and try to argue the relevance of the proposition "if X, then Y." The reality of historical explanation is entirely different; it works the other way round and operates with the proposition "Y exists and may be seen to arise from causal complex A^n, within which complex $X_1 [+ X_2 + X_3 + \ldots]$ may be singled out as more important than the rest." The essence of historical description is unlimited variety; the essence of historical causation is multiplicity. It is this fact which firmly distinguishes it from scientific explanation: *none* of the matters to be explained by the historian ever derives from a single identifiable cause. Everything else follows from this.

Evidently, therefore, the philosophers like Popper,

Hempel, or Mandelbaum, who cannot bear the vagueness (in logic) of the historian's concept of cause and seek to reduce his proceedings to a reliance on general laws—ultimate singlenesses—are furthest from the truth.[18] Thus Popper supposes that the historian deduces the event from its cause and that his explanation must contain "one or more universal laws." The first is wrong; the second sometimes wrong and sometimes right, and nearly always trivial. The first is wrong because the historian does not argue that the fact of A explains the occurrence of B, but instead, possessed of B, seeks in the prehistory of B for circumstances which seem to have given rise to it. After it is over, the process may look like deduction, and in the exposition it may be (though it were better if it were not) displayed in deductive terms, but what actually took place worked inductively from the known conclusion to the causes sought for. The same error spoils even Donagan's point when he argues that a particular explanation is incomplete (though in history acceptable) because the alleged cause could have had other consequences.[19] The historian *knows* his consequences, and to him an explanation involves something that renders the known facts intelligible, not something that could have had only one possible result. Frankel, generally sympathetic to the historian, in the same way rejects explanations "from which it is not possible to deduce exactly what did take place."[20] But this is what no historian either tries or wants to do, nor what he needs to do in order to be properly explanatory. He works from known effect to discoverable cause: the philosopher automatically thinks the other way.

The question of universal laws is more difficult. It is complicated by the fact that some philosophers confuse the laws upon which an explanation rests with the laws that history can be supposed to discover. This confusion underlies Morton White's attempt to deny history any existence at all, on the grounds that the "laws" with which it operates are never specifically historical but "belong" to some other form of study.[21] His argument further embodies a surprising failure to distinguish between content and expression: he will not admit an explanation as historical unless it is framed in words which have only a historical meaning. And lastly he confuses the meaning of "historical" by allowing it only a substantive sense and not an adjectival one: yet what one obviously means by "historical explanation" is an explanation of events in history, not some sort of explanation which is historical in the sense in which impetus offers a physical explanation or osmosis a biological. His whole paper is so peculiarly unsound that one can only wonder at its being taken seriously—until one remembers that he does the great service of replacing history altogether by sociology.[22]

However, even the more sensible and precise theorists of what has been dubbed the "covering-law view"—the view that all explanations contain expressly or implicitly the statement of a general law under which the particular case falls—are unclear about the difference between a law used by the historian and a law discovered by him. The lack of clarity is not surprising: if the historian's explanation rests on a covering law, he may presumably either receive the law from another or provide it for himself from the empirical processes of historical enquiry. Yet the two can be distinguished. The first category contains both the laws of physical reality (including geography and climate, and similar "natural" conditions) and the observed laws of human behavior; the second contains a great number of the modest generalizations to which history is prone (in hereditary monarchies the succession of a minor is liable to produce serious trouble; discontent needs a traumatic experience rather than continuous misery to flare into revolution) and the few "real" laws evolved by deterministic forms of history (the dialectic of the class struggle, the cyclical fate of civilizations). The trouble with the first is that they are either trivial or inadequate; with the first kind of the second that they are not the origin but the conclusion of the explanatory process; and with the last that they have never been proved, being either circular or arbitrarily imposed.

The laws of physical or psychological reality will not serve the purpose of the covering-law theory because on investigation they turn out to offer at best the barest start on an explanation. The historian may be aware (to use examples much used in these discussions) that people like the dust-bowl farmers whose livelihood is threatened by natural disaster will tend to look elsewhere for a better home, or that heavy taxation is unpopular and may in turn render the policy behind it unpopular. These mixtures of natural and psychological "causes" of crashing ordinariness will be accepted because they answer to common experience.[23] They and their like may be at the back of the historian's mind when he comes to investigate situations in which they may be applicable; they can start him in the right direction in his search for an explanation, though experience teaches that ready surrender to these kinds of law produces the superficial accounts which genuine historical work is forever engaged in demolishing. These laws do not explain a particular migration or a particular manifestation of resistance to government action, which must be demonstrated as arising from specific events leading to them before the historian has found an explanation valid to himself. The search for these particulars is not notably assisted by the historian's awareness of such generalizations, nor does his explanation in the end hang on his being able to discover the generalization within or behind it. Moreover, such laws are not in the least predictive in history, the quality demanded of them by the theorists; nothing in particular can be deduced from them because it can easily be shown that, in situations in which they have applied, different results have followed. In similar circumstances, quite as many people in history have stayed where they were and died on the spot as have upped sticks and found new pastures; and heavy taxation has often enough been accepted, sometimes with approval, while the policies behind it have fluctuated in popularity. These covering laws either mean nothing in historical explanation, or are so general and commonplace as to offer nothing useful for the explanation in which they are embedded, or at times can be shown to have worked so differently in their capacity that they cease to be laws.

The laws allegedly derived from historical investigation, usable in turn in explanations, are a rather tired old subject.[24] Very often they are strictly circular: used to "prove" the phenomena from which they are derived. This happened to Marx's doctrine of the class struggle which he proved historically (and falsely) from the so-called bourgeois revolutions of the sixteenth and seventeenth centuries and which has since been used by Marxists to prove the occurrence of that revolution. Alternatively, what may be an attractive explanation in one case—for instance, in the rise and decline of Hellenic civilization—is then turned into a universal, as in Toynbee's theory of civilizations. The case is always proved by improper means: by abstracting artificial (and carefully constructed) "essences" from historical variety. Sometimes the abstraction is more thoughtful and successful than at other times, and such a "law" can then become a fruitful stimulant to explanatory thought. But they are never laws, if only because their stimulating effect as often as not consists in provoking disproof of their applicability. In fact, they can be treated as laws only by doing violence either to facts or to the use of words: Toynbee ignores the fact of the Thirty Years' War when his laws require that the age be one of peace, and Marxist historians

can speak of a centralizing feudalism, even though the one
agreed definition of feudalism must be its production of
decentralized authority, when the scheme demands a feudal
stage while the facts demonstrate an antifeudal stage.
Covering-law theories result either in stressing in an explanation that which is least significant or interesting in it, or
in forcing the event to accommodate itself to the pre-
arranged explanation. That the first is philosophers' nonsense and the second the nonsense of dogmatic historians
does not much affect the issue. Both fail to make sense of
the nature of historical explanation.

It can, in fact, be shown that there can be no laws in
history: that historical analysis cannot discover them and
historical explanation cannot be based on them. An explanatory law may be defined in two ways: it must be falsifiable
by experiment, and it must make prediction possible. That
one cannot conduct historical experiments because one cannot at will re-create identical historical situations is so
familiar a point that I need not labor it. As for prediction,
most people would now agree that a historical explanation, however generalized, at best makes possible a forecast
of probability; the event is forever defying the human passion for knowing the future. There is a useful example in
Gardiner's list: Croce's argument that the lack of every
liberty in the years before 1848 produced "a generation of
acute rebels," turning the minds of students "either to
turbid daydreams . . . or to abstract and simplifying rational-
ism."[25] His description, which is accurate and penetrating
for the 1840's, agrees quite strikingly with any informed
description of the acutely rebellious students of the 1960's
that a dispassionate observer a hundred years hence may
perpetrate. The cause which Croce assigns to the first event,
however, will not work at all for the second. At this
moment, rebelliousness is least acute among students who
live under the most repressive of governments. It could in

fact be argued that the sort of generalized cause which Croce discovered has been prophetically projected: that is to say, the present generation of social leaders has deliberately enlarged the sort of liberty which, Croce has told them from his historical experience, would lead to "the formation of a culture that implies discernment and civilization," only to find no such thing (very far from it) but rather the same result which earlier had allegedly followed upon the absence of such liberty.[26] No doubt the real point is that Croce's explanatory "law" was as inadequate as a mere ascription of present-day rebelliousness to "permissiveness" would be, but the difference between a historical explanation and a predictive law is in any case clear. It is also clear why there must be this difference: the generalized explanation derived from an earlier experience can itself become an element in the situation producing a later experience, with the result that its causal effect is totally altered.

More generally, however, the reason for the failure of historical generalization and explanation to approach the status of a law properly so-called lies in the nature of laws on the one hand and in the nature of the historical event on the other. Laws are either normative or statistical. A normative law is one which says that condition A shall always be followed by condition B—that (to use one of the philosophers' preferred examples) making a billiard ball hit another will cause that other to move in an entirely predictable direction. A statistical law states that after a large number of identical events, the outcome of the next event of the same type is predictable, even though occasional single events of that same kind may produce unpredicted variations. (The development of subatomic physics has changed most scientific laws from normative to statistical.) For practical purposes, statistical laws are as precise as normative ones if the sample is large enough to turn probability into certainty. However, neither kind of law has any meaning in history. Historical events can never be referred

back to a normative law because they are never the product
of a single cause; the product of an infinitely variable
assembly of causes (even supposing that all can be identified) cannot ever be described by the "A is followed by B"
formula. Historical causation differs completely from the
movement of billiard balls. Statistical laws, on the other
hand, cannot apply because historical events are never
sufficiently alike to form the basis of a statistical conclusion. The historian does not deal with identical units sufficient in number to produce a probability approximating to a
certainty; he deals with units (people, facts, events) of a
similarity sufficient to permit limited generalizations, but
no more.[27]

Nevertheless, the concept of a statistical law comes
nearer to the historical reality than that of a normative law;
it is useful in showing why historical generalization is
possible at all and the part it plays in historical explanation.
In one sense, no two things in history are ever alike, at
which level generalization becomes impossible, explanation
ceases, and the historian is reduced to a mindless description of a meaningless sequence of events. No historian, in
fact, is ever satisfied with this—it is not possible to commit
written history to paper on these terms—and the most par-
ticularizing, least generalizing of historians still tries to see
some meaning based on common elements leading to
cautiously phrased and embryonic "statistical laws" which
appear as particular explanations. It is this sort of explanation embodied in the telling of the story which forms the
essence of Gallie's analysis of the problem.[28] The more
analytical historian goes further in the direction of generalizations which, while still not laws in any proper sense,
possess validity beyond the particular explanation. He does
so in the main by abstracting the common elements from
the particular events, ascribing primacy to this or that
common element, and generalizing "statistically" from the
relatively artificial construct so obtained. He can say, for

instance, that a population increase in a given society will, by squeezing available resources, lead to one of three consequences: either it will lead to emigration, or it will call forth an increase in productivity to increase the resources and maintain (or improve) the standard of living, or it will produce a decline in living standards (economic historian's jargon for starvation). If he is any sort of historian, however, he knows that this empirically verifiable *a priori* law is no sort of explanation at all. It is a valid generalization based on historical research, but even in that capacity it is not very useful since it allows for so many separate possibilities (for historical generalizations of the valid kind are always likely to be phrased in this cautious way). Eighteenth-century England experienced the second consequence, eighteenth-century Ireland the third, nineteenth-century Ireland the first. The historian's task has only begun: he must explain why these different consequences of the same "first cause" occurred, and when he tries to do so he finds that the generalization is no help at all. The function of such generalizations approximating to laws is not to explain—he who so uses them produces rubbish—but to define the area within which the historical explanation is to be sought, and sometimes only to press the button which starts the mind thinking. Law-making and the discovery of laws are none of the historian's tasks; law-approximating generalization is not the end of his endeavors but, if useful at all, only the beginning, a fact underlined by the readiness with which the historian borrows such generalizations from other intellectual enterprises. The real problem of historical causation remains, but it remains in a form very different from that posed by the philosophers. The question is not, what part do laws play in historical causes, but how one may account for the event on the basis of empirical enquiry.

At this point, the more perceptive answers given by Dray and Gardiner, who—whatever their differences—both ques-

tion absolute "covering-law" theories, are more helpful; but
they must be admitted to lack cogency. Although Gardiner
asserts that the conflict between materialistic (law based)
and idealistic (reenacting) theories of history is illusory,[29]
he accepts some of the less convincing aspects of the latter
too readily. He was bemused by Collingwood, as many of us
were between fifteen and twenty years ago. This unreal and
unrealistic notion that the historian understands history by
reenacting it in his mind, backed up by the fatal suggestion
that ideas are the only realities in history, has had some
very disturbing consequences, from the conviction that no
history is worth writing except intellectual history to the
opinion that history is just what the historian dreams up.
Gardiner, though not an idealist in the full Croce-Colling-
wood sense, is not immune. He will not have it that an
assessment of motive based on the historian's experience
involves the historian's experience being transformed into
that of the historical person considered (a good common-
sensical warning, and a true analysis of historical research), but he nevertheless supposes that the historian
need not produce any more than a convincing description
of motive—convincing, that is, in terms of human experience—which leaves us once again back inside the mind of
Collingwood's historian. This counsel of moderate despair
opens the way to a purely relativist view of historical explanation: the historian's word must be accepted on trust
(he knows the man, his time, and what he could do) or
rejected (how can he know?), with nothing to guide the
judgment except a vague sort of weighing up of the possibilities. Gardiner's analysis of extrahuman causes in history is
no more conclusive. What is so patently missing here is
practical experience of the effect of historical evidence (the
relics of the past) on the investigating mind. Not without
reason did Collingwood do his historical work in a period
exceptionally devoid of evidence.

Dray similarly seeks to resolve the dilemma created by

the fact that historical explanation will not fit into a theory of laws by setting up a category of "how" explanations by the side of the more usual "why" explanations.[30] He holds that in some contexts the need for an explanation "is satisfactorily met if what happens is merely shown to have been *possible*" and will even admit into the category of explanations a mere demonstration that an event "need not have caused surprise." The first point offends the first principle of historical explanation: that which we try to explain is never possible, it always *is,* and even if Dray meant to say that it is enough for the historian to offer an explanation in which the cause of the known effect is possible rather than certain (an inversion which, I think, he did not have in mind), he is a long way from giving an account of historical explanation which is either precise or useful. As for the second point, one must ask, surprise to whom? Why should we accept another man's assurance that there was nothing surprising about an event unless we are to surrender to his supposed standing as an authority? Yet if he is to claim authority he must first demonstrate an understanding not based on mere personal assertion. And if he is to do that, and if he has to convince us of the unsurprising nature of the event, he must assuredly investigate causes—that is, ask the question why.

Possibly I do Gardiner and Dray an injustice; it may well be that, untrained in philosophy as I am, I misunderstand their reasoning. At least I find their treatment in general much more acceptable (much more like the reality familiar to me as a historian) than the arguments of the Popper-Hempel school or of those who fall back on symbolic logic —the discipline furthest removed from either life or history —in discussing the problems of historical understanding.[31] With these I have no qualms in saying that I do see what they are getting at and think them quite mistaken. On the other hand, Dray in particular, but also Danto and Gallie, come much closer to understanding what it is his-

torians actually do. Nevertheless, the fact that even Dray
ends up with such spectacular relativist and personal results must give pause. Enough people do suppose that in
the end all historical explanation is subjective, and (as I
have shown) the attempts to get round this by interpreting
explanations as deductively derived from universal laws
break down. Yet, as I have tried to argue elsewhere from the
experience of writing and reading history for twenty years,
this relativism plays much less part in the reality of the
historian's enterprise than the legend has it, and convincing
objectivity in the account needs no aid from *a priori* constructs.[32]

I agree that there are limits to the degree to which historians can be precise and avoid subjective answers, but the
doubtful area is much smaller than such arguments as those
Gardiner and Dray suppose. And the reason for their failure
to assimilate the cases they have in mind when they wish
to be content with the probable and the personal into a
structure of precise causality is also plain; it has already
been stated. They are still philosophers, working from the
cause to the effect, from the circumstances to the possible
consequences. The historian, to say it again, is bound to
work from the effect to the cause. The event once established, he explains it by working backward, even if in
writing he tells it forward; and he does so from a rigorous
position defined by his evidence. The evidence never sup-
plies all the answers or complete answers; it always leaves
something to the interpreting mind; but it so severely controls the range of possibilities as to give the resultant explanation objective cogency. If the evidence does not delimit
the area of explanations sufficiently, the historian must
admit this; he may state a preference, but unless he can
demonstrate it from evidence he must describe it for what
it is—a guess. The first condition attendant upon explanations in history, and one which sharply differentiates them
from explanations in the sciences, is that they are not

always to be got and that this deficiency arises from the subject matter itself, not from the insufficiencies of the enquirer. In history, things cannot always be explained.

Still, as a rule causality lies at the heart of historical reconstruction; it cannot be abandoned without depriving historical enquiry of purpose and history as written of intelligibility.[33] It does not become amenable to scientific demonstration and creates no conditions for prediction, but it makes possible explanations for the course of events which will rest on cohesive empirical demonstration and satisfy the understanding. When we ask why, and are answered because, we know whether or not we have received an explanation, though it should be remembered that in history the because very often remains open to refinement, refutation, or variation. Thanks to the absence or confusion of evidence, some historical questions cannot be so treated, but these are not enough to destroy the place of cause and motive in historical reconstruction. The search for causes is legitimate, even necessary, and such obtuse objections as were raised, for instance, by Barraclough need not impress. What does matter is that the search should be conducted properly. Even more important than an investigation into what the historian might mean by talking about causes is a morphology of causes, an attempt to classify and range them: At the very least, it is time to put an end to futile debates which worry whether "the cause" of the Reformation was the decay of the Church or Luther's protest against indulgences, "the cause" of World War I the murder of the archduke or the arms race. A firm conviction of the propriety of the search for causes is particularly necessary if we are to avoid the frequent eruptions of the conspiracy theory of history, the theory that something happened because some wicked man or men meant it to happen.

What, then, does a historian mean by causes? He means

those antecedent events, actions, thoughts, and situations
which can be proved, by demonstration and inference, to
have influenced the coming about of the event which he is
trying to explain. In order to discover them, he works from
the event to be explained (*explanandum*) to the explaining
events (*explanans*); that is, he deduces the cause, not
the consequences. This he does not only in the course of
working out, inasmuch as he starts with the *explanandum*
already known and the *explanans* still to be discovered, but
also (as a rule) in his presentation of the result, especially
if he is writing analytical rather than narrative history. An
ideal narrative of the Reformation, for instance, might describe the century before 1517 in such a way that the
schism in the Church emerged unsurprisingly at the right
chronological point—unsurprisingly, that is, even for
readers who have never heard of the Reformation. This,
however, is not really possible: neither historians nor their
readers are ever in the position of the audience at the first
night of *Hamlet*, with no idea of the outcome, since the
essence of historical knowledge is hindsight.[34] In effect, all
histories of the Reformation are bound to start by stating
or assuming the fact of the schism and then present its
causes. Even if the narrative begins with a description of
the event's prehistory, it can be relevant and useful only
if it consistently remembers the event to be explained and
still to be mentioned. Whether or not the logic of causal
explanation requires that the consequence be deductible
from the cause, the practice of historical writing always
requires that the cause be referable to the effect. This is
important (as we have seen) because it abolishes uni-
versality in the statement of historical causes.

The definition which I have offered contains three elements that require further discussion: the kind of causes
admitted by the historian, the nature of the causal effect,
and the standards of proof necessary.

Historical causes (events, actions, thought, and situations) divide into two distinct categories: (1) those providing conditions for the production of a given event which I will call situational causes, and (2) those directly productive of it. The latter again subdivide into (a) intentional causes (when the producer willed the product), and (b) unintentional causes; these last further subdivide into (i) those where an act of will produced unintended results, and (ii) those in which no act of will was involved.

Not every historical event must be preceded by examples of all these types of causes, but a really large or complex event derives from them all. This may be illustrated, once again, by means of the Reformation. The *explanandum* is the permanent (well, so far permanent) division of the single Latin Church of Rome into rival denominations. Causes of type (1) have been plentifully identified: the state of the Church, nationalist resentment of Italian popes, spiritual dissatisfaction, the growth of humanism and criticism of official learning, the desire for ecclesiastical wealth, and so forth. Type (2a) is represented by such acts as Luther's three revolutionary treatises of 1520, Zwingli's preaching for a reform in 1523, or Thomas Cromwell's program of a political break with Rome. To type (2bi) belong Luther's theses against indulgences, Erasmus' edition of the New Testament, or Henry VIII's desire for a divorce from his first wife; while type (2bii) includes such facts as Charles V's involvement in the Spanish rebellion or the separatist ambitions of the German princes.[35] The type (1) causes are characterized by one general quality: neither singly nor together did they create a condition in which the Reformation was bound to happen. In the standard sense, they did not *cause* it at all; there is certainly no "if A then B" character about them. Nevertheless, from the point of view of historical hindsight, it is clear that by their existence they allowed or encouraged the type (2) causes to bring about the particular historical result, and to deny the name of causes to them would be not only pedantic but thoroughly misleading. The type (2) causes, on the other hand, can be shown to have directly induced consequences which are part of the historical event called the Reformation.

While the historian, in seeking causal explanations, must always endeavor to discover causes of all the types listed, he must be careful to discriminate in his treatment of them. There has long been a tendency to regard type (1) causes as somehow more deep, more distinguished, more worthy of the serious historian, altogether more professionally respectable, largely because they are usually more complex and less attached to individual actors. This distinction by quality—as more or less important—does not help very much, as the familiar and sterile discussions about which cause of this or that matters most show well enough. Historians would be well advised to stop thinking in these terms of the profound and the superficial; instead they should assemble and consider the whole complex. What really matters is that situational causes cannot by themselves result in any particular event at all; to put it the other way round, they are capable of producing a very large range of possible results. Thus the historian who identifies only type (1) causes has not explained his event. None of the situational conditions which have been identified or may yet be identified as "leading to" the Reformation in fact led to it: none could at the time be regarded as productive of a schism (or were so thought of), nor could any historian equipped with knowledge of them alone predict or infer the Reformation from them. On the other hand, type (2) —direct—causes do produce obvious and particular effects, or rather, particular events spring obviously from identifiable type (2) causes. Yet if a historian of the Reformation were possessed of all conceivable direct causes and nothing else, he could not possibly either understand or explain why the agglomerate of all the events and their causes before him should have become transformed into so large and complex and influential a consequence as the Reformation clearly was. In order to understand why his direct causes operated as they did, he must acquaint himself with causes of the situational type.

Both the nature of historical causation and the historian's task in explaining events should now be plain. All historical events are the products of causes of both types. Direct causes explain why the event actually happened; situational causes explain why direct causes proved effective and why the event occupies a particular place in the historical picture and story, both as an effect and as a cause of further effects. The differences between the two types together with the inescapable presence of both explain why historical explanation cannot be determinist. Situational causes explain only why certain consequential possibilities may result; in the particular they become significant only through the presence of direct causes. On the other hand, direct causes have the particular effects discoverable only because they work in circumstances conditioned by situational causes. The individual event is the product of a particular complex of causes of both types, a complex in which every ingredient is variable. If it were possible to reconstruct an identical complex, identical and predictable results would no doubt follow; but, as has already been pointed out, constructing an identical "experiment" means among other things eliminating all knowledge of the previous "experiment" and its outcome, which means that the thing can be done only by someone who has no knowledge of what he is trying to do. Identical events in history are therefore not only an idle speculation because of the great variety of variables, but are in logic impossible. Variation is further increased by the fact that, apart from the multi-

tude of variable elements, the degrees of variation in each
are infinite and react upon one another. Hindsight makes
it possible to say that the condition of Europe in 1517
favored a breaking up of the religious unity, but if Luther
had not started his attack in 1517, the event we know as
the Reformation would still not have happened. If someone
else had attacked indulgences, or if Luther had done so in
1520 (to take only two quite minor variations from the
historical fact), the outcome would have been quite different—unpredictably different. The nature of the only causes
which the historian is able and qualified to discover bars
any but the vaguest and most conjectural forecasts, while
it makes possible perfectly accurate retrospective explanations of events.

This predicament is further underlined by the precise
nature of the causal effect which can be discovered in
history. It is not the same as the effect of causes in such a
science as physics where a specific action leads to a specific
reaction. No historical cause ever *must have* a given known
effect, namely, the historical event to be explained. The best
that the historian can say is that it *did have* that effect.
This is so because neither of the two types of causes described can do more than influence the course of events in
the direction discovered by empirical enquiry. We can say
that Luther's three treatises evoked a revolutionary reponse,
and we can (from situational causes) explain why this was
so. We cannot say that they were bound to do so—in no
single instance can an individual's reaction to reading the
treatises be predicted or assumed—and we can throughout
discover elements in the story which worked the other way
but which, usually for assignable reasons, failed to operate.
These are the "ifs" of history: if Charles V had been able
to attend to the German problem before 1521, if the elector
of Saxony had not been persuaded to protect Luther, if the
humanists had sooner understood the fundamental differ-

ence between Luther's revolution and their own, and so on. These ifs are more than idle toys because they emphasize the tenuous, often seemingly accidental, element in the chain of historical causation and prevent (or should prevent) the historian from mistaking proof of causation for necessity or inevitability. By highlighting decisive moments or decisive crossing points in the story, they may also enable him to arrive more accurately at what causes did actually operate. Remembering that his causes do not so much produce results as make results possible, even probable, and remembering that they can never be identified as causes of a given result until that result has occurred, should stop the historian from ever saying that only one course of events was possible—that what did happen was bound to happen. He cannot say this because of necessity he seeks causes for known events (for what did happen) and does not identify events as causes of yet unknown consequences; and because the causes he discovers should be described not as bringing about a given result but as influencing the manifestation of a given result. This last point is more obvious for situational causes which can never be said to do anything else, but it is, on reflection, true also of direct causes whose effect becomes clear only after the event.

With causes so tricky in their operation, one would naturally expect a high standard of proof, as well as great difficulties in obtaining it. Here we run into a curious situation: we get neither help nor hindrance from the philosophers. The whole elevated discussion has gone on about problems of explanation without a single sign that the historian is required to do more than allege his causes. None of the thinkers who have argued this business at such length seem to have concerned themselves with proof, so much so that the word does not even occur in their indexes. And yet the possibility of explaining historical events depends far less on the kind of causes the historian works with than on whether he can show them to have been causes at all. It is here that he differs most obviously from the natural scientist who can prove the correctness of his causal chain by repeating it experimentally at will or demonstrating it by the rigorous methods of mathematical logic. He can also verify by inversion or falsification, by showing that the absence of a cause would result in the absence of an effect. The historian can do none of these things, least of all the last, however fond some historians may be of arguing that if only this or that had not happened, or been done differently, events would have taken a predictably different turn.[36] All he can do is to work positively and particularly, that is to say, show in given cases that an effect was produced by a cause.

What, then, constitutes proof in historical explanations? The rigorous answer is that an explanation in history is proved if it can be demonstrated, from historical evidence, that a given cause A exercised influence in producing effect B. This statement is not as tautological as at first sight it may appear, but applied rigorously it limits the area of *provable* causes quite severely. In fact, it limits it to type (2) causes. Historical evidence makes possible the demonstration, to continue with our chosen example, that willed actions had intended effects: people's reaction to reading Luther's works can be told from evidence, and when Zwingli's sermons calling for an end to popery are followed by the introduction of the Reformation in Zürich his activities can rigorously be described as a cause. The argument holds also for the other type (2) causes: thus the proof is solid which demonstrates that the troubles in Spain prevented Charles V from attending to Luther and left the imperial authorities unable to arrest the spread of the Lutheran revolt through Germany.[37] For such direct causes, evidence usually exists, though not always because so much historical evidence is simply missing. It always exists *in posse,* and rigorous demonstration can be demanded when direct causes are being alleged. The notorious problem of tracing the influence of one writer upon another may be solvable by evidence, as when we have a definite statement or citation proving that Mr. X read Mr. Y; but the need of rigorous proof renders problematic a mere inference from the fact that Y's ideas occur in X's writings. This may be a case of straight borrowing or influence, but the possibility always exists (and in fact frequently occurs) that two people thinking about the same problems will come up with very similar answers. However, what matters is that for direct causes it is theoretically always possible to construct a strict chain of proof resting on historical evidence; for these causes, the demand for such a demonstration is therefore always justified, and the historian, frustrated by the lacunae in the evidence, must remember to distinguish between the direct causes he has really proved, those where he has set up a very strong presumption of validity, and those he has been forced to conjecture.

Situational causes of type (1) are in this respect quite different. The proof here required neither can nor need be so precise and demonstrable. It cannot be so because, as has been said, these causes do not have the same formal causal relationship with the *explanandum.* It can never be shown from evidence that, for instance, the weakness of central authority in Germany and the splintered political organization of the country's territories (themselves phenomena which can be fully described from the evidence) produced the particular effects which these situations are agreed to have had on the Reformation. But neither need this be demonstrated since all that is demanded of such causes is that they should have produced a situation in which the actual course of events became possible, encourageable, or (if one so wishes) even very likely. For type

(1) causes, the needs of proof are therefore satisfied if it can be demonstrated, from historical evidence, that the constellation of forces or state of mind produced could have influenced events in the direction which actually occurred. It should be stressed that the discovery and identification of situational causes cannot, by their nature, be based on a logical chain of reasoning; it must be intuitive. What the historian does is to consider the prehistory and presituation of his given event and situation; in them he discovers elements which, he thinks, influenced subsequent events (his *explanandum*) in a positive or negative way. This does not, however, absolve him from demonstrating, by means of historical evidence, both the existence of his intuited cause and the manner in which it contributed to the subsequent situation. He must be able to show that the splintering of Germany made possible the disruption of the Church (for instance, by subjecting the Church's members to secular control), or that humanist attacks on the old learning created a readiness to quarrel with the authority of the Church. All this he can do, by the rigorous canons of historical study; what he cannot do is to show from evidence that either situational cause produced Luther's protest or the support for it from other people; nor need he do this. Type (1) causes must be shown, rigorously, to have produced situations, not events.

In practice, these standards of rigor need relaxing a trifle. Historical evidence is always patchy and for some periods very thin indeed. The historian who confined himself to analyzing or telling stories in which he could strictly (in the manner here laid down) prove every assertion or explanation would write very little history and very restricted history; in fact, those historians who are skeptical of anything not proven rigorously do write very little. One may respect such upright behavior, provided it is not associated with envy of the more fluent, but one may also deplore the consequences if they amount to silence. Historical narrative and explanation must therefore be less absolute in their demands: they must admit the conjectural and the possible, elements which escape from the net of strict demonstration and open the door to unending argument. But while such imprecision must distress the philosopher and the scientist, it need not trouble the historian to whom, indeed, it constitutes the special excitement of his craft. Yet there are limits: the historian who produces a stream of might-have-beens and must-have-beens deserves to lose credit. There ought to be means for distinguishing between legitimate and wild speculation, and so there are. They are these two: proof must be produced where possible, nor must statements be made which can be precisely disproved, and second, the causes alleged must be probable in terms of the people and situations involved.

The first is obvious and needs no further exposition, except to stress that much bad history is written by people who, aware that they are entitled to conjecture beyond the evidence, cheerfully conjecture where the evidence exists. Only the historian who has proved his rigor where rigor is possible deserves trust when deficiencies in the evidence or special complications in the story force him to be less rigorous. The second, however, needs a word. What I have in mind is, I know, so far from rigorously provable that it may be thought very dangerous in practitioners of a supposedly exact craft: reconstructions and explanations based on the visualizing of situations in terms which are "real" though not provable in detail. Perhaps it is this sort of thing that may have encouraged Popper and Hempel to adhere to their false analysis of universal laws in historical explanation. Especially when he considers people's motives, the historian is often forced to argue beyond the evidence: what goes on in the mind is rarely documented.[38] Why people did things may have to be inferred from what they

did and what they were. In this task, the historian's con-
trolling element will be, on the one hand, an understanding
of human behavior and motivation in general, and of the
realities of the man's time and place on the other. The first
may be treated as amounting to a form of universal law, if
one insists on having these, though it is so universal and
wide (comprehensive) as to have little legislative force and
no specific usefulness until applied to a sizeable body of
particular circumstances. The second is the historian's
peculiar contribution to this reconstruction: even more
than a proper search for and treatment of evidence, which
up to a point can be taught, it distinguishes the real and
successful historian from the kind of substitute that the
layman finds so hard to recognize. The quality of the man
and his mind do become very important here: these controls upon unsound speculation are not perfect, but in the
right hands—in the hands of the trained and natural historian—they suffice to produce unextravagant conjectures
which, if accompanied in the rest of the story by the necessary elements of rigor and evidence-based proof, give
authority to his explanation.

An example will show how this works. In the years
1529–1534 two men were working their way up in the
service of King Henry VIII: Stephen Gardiner and Thomas
Cromwell. The first began ahead of the other, then fell well
behind, but came to the fore again after Cromwell's fall
and death in 1540. Their careers in office and in the king's
favor can be fully and properly documented. Much is correctly demonstrable about their personalities—Gardiner the
bishop and diplomatist, writer, and defender of his order,
irascible and rash but also intellectually distinguished and
capable of generous friendship; Cromwell the layman and
administrator, policy-maker and radical reformer, drastic
and often ruthless, with a circle of close personal friends
and a wider circle of close personal enemies. Yet the evi-

dence that they were rivals and that Gardiner took the lead in overthrowing Cromwell is not primary and permits of no perfect proof. Apart from some near-contemporary comment (from John Foxe, the martyrologist), it is strictly inferential; their own correspondence, for instance, shows nothing but a straightforward business relationship with touches of mutual appreciation. However, it can be shown that Cromwell acquired a crucial office which Gardiner had held, just after a known false step in policy had for a time lost Gardiner the king's favor; that throughout Cromwell's ascendancy Gardiner was rarely at court and often on embassy abroad; and that the issues of the final crisis (final for Cromwell) resolved themselves into a victory for the views known to have been held by Gardiner and a defeat for those known to have been held by Cromwell. From all this, the historian may, quite legitimately and without any risk of rashness, conclude the fact of their rivalry, and— applying a generalized understanding of the ways of the human mind to the known facts of the rivals' characters— may fairly infer the existence of jealousy and resentment on Gardiner's side, manifestations which in turn came to play an important causal role in the fall of Cromwell. The feelings and motives ascribed to Gardiner are not provable from the evidence, nor are they in any way peculiar to the historical setting; but the "laws" of human behavior are here in no way contradicted by the known facts which rather corroborate the conclusions based on these "laws." As for the argument that this search for motive is superfluous and historically uninteresting, especially since conjecture must enter into it, the truth is that without an understanding of what Gardiner was up to, and why, the crisis of 1540 would not properly be explained. In this instance, the reconstruction of story, causes, and motives, compounded of proven detail and conjectured detail and in accord with a generalized understanding of how men be-

have, may claim the certainty of an established case; and
the example is in fact typical of the way in which historical
explanation, always complex and mixed, invariably works
in practice.

Now, of course, the danger in all this is that historians
may too readily resort to an illegitimate use of their necessary speculation and imagination. The error can take the
form of explanatory categories given no meaning, as when
some specific actions or thoughts are derived from national
or racial character. Or it can appear in a refusal to adjust
the "universal law" to the historical condition, the most
familiar manifestation of which is the issue of moral judg-
ments in history, an issue I do not propose to concern myself with here. A less obvious example is provided by Professor Trevor-Roper who, in a work of his youth, refused
to contemplate the possibility that the eminent men of the
seventeenth century really "tortured and executed less conventional believers solely to please God" or that people
really fought over doctrines. His understanding of human
nature convinced him that those men, like those of the
1930's, were really moved by motives of political and economic self-interest. Allowing for the bit of truth in the
observation and all reservations made around it, and despite
the massive research producing proven statements throughout the book, this erroneous use of the situational generalization—erroneous just because it refuses the real seventeenth-century situation entry into the argument—haunts
the work throughout.[39] This is a subtle case; obvious examples of a rash and even frivolous ascription of conjectured motives and causes can be found only too readily.
Gardiner's thirteen examples, already analyzed, contain no
fewer than five (nos. 4, 5, 6, 8, 10) which one can only
deplore.[40] It is always necessary to remain alert in question-
ing one's own and other people's identification of causes.

This need, however, is not based solely on the possibility

of error. It is good history as well as bad that compels continued skepticism, and the reason for this lies at the heart of historical causality as here analyzed. As has been shown, all historical events are the products of a complex of "causes," some of which cannot be proved in any strict sense. In consequence, all historical explanations remain up to a point provisional, or at least subject to the possibility of alteration as either increased knowledge or subtler understanding suggests better explanations. There are very few questions in history, above the level of the absolutely simple, on which it is not possible to learn more, and to the reflective historian this should constitute one of the great attractions of his craft. But men also like certainties and firm ground (of which history, let it be said, contains quite a lot, too), and the danger is that their reluctance to accept the necessary conditions of their chosen trade may incline some historians to elevate conjectured probability into agreeable certainty. Hence the search for historical law. Danto is right when he says that "the discovery of historical laws would in no degree support the prophetic pretensions of substantive philosophers of history,"[41] nor (I may add) of determinist writers of history, either. What is more, historical laws—even if ever discovered, even if they could in fact exist—seem very unlikely to explain even the past. Take the case of a familiar assertion which comes as near to being a historical law of relative precision as may be devised, a law derived from historical experience and in turn applicable to the historical event. I mean the generalization that revolutions occur not when the revolutionary elements in a society are worst off, but rather when their condition has in any case started to improve. This generalization can be supported with sufficient historical examples: the condition of the Third Estate in France before 1789, the beginnings of constitutionalism in prerevolutionary Russia, even perhaps (*minima cum maximis*) the posi-

tion of university students on the eve of the revolt of
"student power." In each case, the carriers of revolution
were better off than they had been when they seemed at
rest, and the generalization may well have enough truth in
it to be treated as a historical law. Yet what use is this
law? It certainly makes possible no prediction of forth-
coming revolutions: no one can, by analyzing a potentially
revolutionary element in society and finding it experiencing
relative betterment, conclude that it will revolt, let alone at
what point it will do so. What is more, the "law" in no way
assists in explaining the revolutions from which it has been
deduced. In the complex prehistory of the French or Rus-
sian Revolutions, with their mixture (as hindsight sees it)
of situational and direct causes relevant to the later event,
the facts that the lot of the bourgeois was improving or that
Russia at last had a constitution stand out as least meaningful of all.

The historian needs to concern himself with causes and
motives, and the political historian, telling a story of
change and struggle, can least avoid that search for antecedents which has at times been regarded as particularly
fruitless, especially by those who think they have abolished
it by substituting structural analysis for narrative account.
(Like any other critic of the concept of cause, they have
changed only the name, not the reality.) But while the task
needs to be discharged, its problems should not be overlooked. The conditions of historical study—the nature of
the subject matter, the state of the evidence, and the purposes of reconstruction—all make sure that while a very
high degree of cogent probability can usually be achieved
in explaining the occurrence of a historical event, the area
of reasonable conjecture remains large enough to demand
the continuation of argument and debate. Universal laws,
whether derived from other studies or from history itself,
offer either no help or at best the most marginal. The

particular event is especially particular in its causes. But one may end with the consoling reflection that the philosophical problems in analyzing the historian's exceptionally complicated activity are a great deal more intractable than that activity itself turns out to be for him who tries it. Discovering causes and explaining events is not the hardest of the historian's tasks.

NOTES

1. E.g. P. Gardiner, *The Nature of Historical Explanation* (Oxford, 1952); W. H. Dray, *Laws and Explanation in History* (Oxford, 1957); M. Mandelbaum, "Historical Explanation and the Problem of 'Covering Laws,'" *History and Theory* 1 (1961): 229–242; A. Donagan, "Historical Explanation: the Popper-Hempel Theory Reconsidered," *History and Theory* 4 (1965): 3–26 (with useful bibliography); W. B. Gallie, *Philosophy and Historical Understanding* (London, 1964), ch. 5; A. C. Danto, *Analytical Philosophy of History* (Cambridge, 1965), chs. 10 and 11.

An important collection of papers was edited by P. Gardiner under the title *Theories of History* (New York, 1959); see esp. pp. 344–475 (hereinafter cited as *Theories*). Since writing this chapter, I have read Gordon Leff's *History and Social Theory* (London, 1969) which contains a long discussion of some of the matters here handled. While Dr. Leff and I are agreed in many respects, some of our differences reflect the different experiences of a historian of ideas and the sort of political historian who works with manuscript sources. I think that Dr. Leff has allowed himself to be too much impressed by some—especially sociological—theory; his useful stress on the contingent in history makes him overlook the fact that though many things always *can* happen, only the known event actually occurred. That is to say, I would argue that historians and their conclusions are markedly less at the influence of what is contingent to them than anyone specializing in the history dealing with men's ideas only would seem willing to agree, and that therefore in most areas of historical study the grounds for gaining understanding and expressing the explanation are firmer and less affected by the historian's personal contribution than Dr. Leff can accept.

2. *Theories*, p. 403.

3. *Theories*, pp. 432, 441. Williamson on the Danes and Norsemen equals some scientific journalist on heredity or relativity.

4. *History and Theory* 4 (1965): 2–22.

5. Gardiner, *Historical Explanation*, p. 135.

6. *Theories*, p. 419.

7. For a good summary of the case, cf. Leff, *History and Social Theory*, ch. 9.

8. *Theories*, pp. 440–441.

9. Gardiner, *Historical Explanation*, pp. 65–67.

10. Below, pp. 129ff.

11. *Theories*, pp. 370–371.

12. This position is taken up throughout Leff's treatment of explanation in his *History and Social Theory*.

13. Presidential address to the Historical Association, delivered on April 12, 1966; published, Historical Association, London, 1967.

14. Cf. my *Practice of History* (London and New York, 1967), p. 101. Dr. Leff (*History and Social Theory*, p. 69) wishes to retain the term. He does not say why.

15. Hempel found support for his belief that all historical explanations embody a universal law ("The Function of General Laws in History," *Theories*, p. 344ff.) in the use of such terms as class struggle, vested interest, tendency to conspicuous consumption (*Theories*, p. 350). No doubt; but this is so because terms such as these are meaningless in themselves, being summaries (inevitably at least slightly misleading summaries) of complicated *assemblies* of causes. They are, in fact, in the same category as the nonexplanations like "mission in history" or "predestined fate" which Hempel rightly scorns (*Theories*, p. 347); being derived from the constructs of economists rather than theologians gives them no better standing among historians.

16. For the argument that it is an error, see my *Practice of History*, esp. ch. 2. On the study of historians see *Practice of History*, p. 154, and above, pp. 78–79. The argument for abandoning the notion of cause altogether is most authoritatively stated in Michael Oakeshott, *Experience and Its Modes* (Cambridge, 1933). Of late, the historiographical analysis of history has even penetrated into the textbooks: see the interesting, sometimes illuminating, sometimes rather perverse attempt to write general history around the characters of earlier historians in Norman F. Cantor, *The English* (vol. 1 only so far: New York, 1967).

17. Above, ch. 1, n. 26.

18. The clearest statement of this position is Hempel's much cited paper on "The Function of General Laws in History," *Theories*, p. 344ff. This is quite exceptionally devoid of serious historical examples or any apparent understanding of the actual tasks involved in explaining historical events. For a useful review of these law-centered positions, see Donagan in *History and Theory* 4 (1965): 3ff. Surprisingly, C. B. McCullagh, who does know much better what the writing of history means and justly attacks the view that narrative is by itself sufficient explanation ("Narrative and Explanation in History," *Mind* 78 [1969]: 256–261) seems to accept Hempel's demand that even in history causes are not so unless they are predictive.

19. *Theories*, p. 434.

20. *Theories*, p. 411.

21. *Theories*, pp. 357ff. E.g., when the historian uses a discovery of psychology to explain a piece of history, he is not offering a historical explanation. The argument would deprive all nonphysical sciences of their existence.

22. It is rather nice to find that the reprint of White's paper in *Theories* itself serves to produce the sort of confusion which historians are trained to disentangle. It is stated to have been first published in 1943 (p. 357); yet in the text, White speaks of President Truman and the atom bomb, an event of 1945 (p. 358). Does the discrepancy arise from his "slight" revisions intended "to eliminate certain awkward passages and to state certain points more clearly" (p. 370)? This would seem an inadequate description of the revision if that included the insertion of the Truman argument.

23. I agree here with Dray, *Laws*, p. 18ff.

24. The modest generalizations referred to above require no further discussion; no one would in fact treat them as laws in the covering-law sense.

25. Gardiner, *Historical Explanation*, p. 66, example 3.

26. I am not suggesting that Croce's remark is the direct cause of present-day social attitudes.

27. See Dray's quite correct argument that the logician's attempt to subsume the specific circumstances of the historian's explanation under the guise of a law simply leads to a constantly enlarged particularization of the so-called "law" which ends at infinity (*Laws*, pp. 33–35). The ultimate and only right answer, then, is that there is a separate law explaining every separate event (set of events) for which an explanation is sought; but a law which states that, on condition that ten or twenty or more defined variables happen, a particular result can be deduced or predicted, is a law only by favor of logic's desire for laws.

28. Gallie's development of Oakeshott's suggestion that the story, as it were, explains itself, into the view that historical explanation equals the telling of the story (*Philosophy and the Historical Understanding*) underestimates the difficult complexity of explaining by narrating. In order to explain, narrative needs to contain a great deal of explicit analysis and argument, difficult to write (see my *Practice of History*, pp. 137–140) but even more difficult to subject to logical analysis. See below, p. 180, n. 6.

29. Gardiner, *Historical Explanation*, p. 136.

30. *Laws*, p. 156ff.

31. Gert Müller, "History as a Rigorous Discipline," *History and Theory* 6 (1967): 299ff.

32. *Practice of History*, pp. 51ff., 96ff.

33. I ought perhaps to come to grips with Oakeshott's famous elimination of cause from history (see above, n. 16). He maintained that description of change equals explanation of change, and he held that what links events in history are not cause and effect but a kind of coexistence in which they are "intrinsically related." These views have been fruitful in philosophy, but they are hard to reconcile with what one does in writing history. I agree with Dray (*Laws*, p.

112ff.) that Oakeshott created his dilemma by a needlessly idiosyncratic view of cause (as though it were a physical third linking two events) rather than a description of the relationship of two events: exploded notions of the ether offer a better metaphor for the mutual effects of events in history than quantum mechanics do.

34. This is true even of so-called contemporary history which, in fact, is always very recent history. The historian's knowledge of the outcome is there more limited and uncertain than it is for more distant events, but some he must have or he would not be able to treat the subject historically at all.

35. It will be seen that causes in which no act of will is involved can include manifestations of human purpose; the question is whether the act of will had any specific reference to the event investigated. *The comuneros* "willed" the discomfiture of Charles V's government but not the fact that he was thereby hindered from stopping Luther, yet the second was as much caused by their actions as the first. The category to which a cause is assigned depends on the consequence considered: as causes in history are never single, so few things had only one identifiable effect.

36. The "new economic history" has tried to elevate this dubious method into a scientific tool called counterfactual analysis, but with no success in showing that changing parameters in their progressions does not remove the argument from the realm of history into that of arbitrary fantasy. See, e.g., R. W. Fogel in *Economic History Review*, 2nd Series, 19 (1966): 642ff.

37. I am not suggesting that there were not additional reasons for the imperial authorities' ineffectiveness.

38. Motives may, however, be documented, for instance in letters or memoirs or the assessment of others; and though such evidence is usually confused, the instruments of historical criticism can often achieve a high degree of precision in reconstructing them.

39. H. R. Trevor-Roper, *Archbishop Laud* (London, 1940), especially pp. 1–2. Of course, writing in 1939, the author failed to appreciate how much purely doctrinal squabbles had to do with the political troubles of the 1930's, and equally of course, his later work shows him to have changed his mind somewhat on the meaning of these "universals."

40. Gardiner, *Historical Explanation*, pp. 65–67.

41. Danto, *Analytical Philosophy*, p. 254.

CHAPTER 5

The End Product

Political history, then, retains its place, or at least a proper place, in the study of the past. It deals with matters of continuing importance; the objections to pursuing it do not convince; the relics of the past tend to make it the main part of the story that can be told; and it is justified in employing methods involving a search for consequential links between events through the passage of time. Above all, it has the advantage of being interesting, amusing, and exciting—or at any rate, it can be all those things, whereas other forms of historical study find it difficult to descend from the occasionally tedious plane of high seriousness. Political history will do well not to take itself too seriously; political historians who cannot see the funny side of public life would do better to immerse themselves in the thick molasses of social history. Traditional and even a trifle old-fashioned though this concern with politics may well be, dead it is not. A good deal of the history still to be discovered and told is still political, and not only in recent history where obviously the advance of time continuously enlarges the area to be worked. Especially, whenever history is a story, that story is liable to revolve around issues of public affairs, great and small. Narrative history is usually political history because narrative records movement, and the dynamic life of society (as I have stressed several times) equals political life.

To many people, especially among those whose interest in history is neither professional nor creative, the predominance of narrative will in itself prove attractive. Readers like a good story, and historians ought to like a good story better than they—so many of them—do. All the history that has caught the general imagination is, in fact, narrative. Gibbon on the fall of Rome, Macaulay on the English Revolution, Trevelyan on the adventures of Garibaldi, and lesser practitioners by the dozen all attract because they tell good stories and tell them well. What is more, their ability to do this even overcomes other deficiencies: one continues to read, and justly to admire work of this sort without necessarily thinking it accurate, reliable, or useful in illuminating the past. The popularity of biography[1]* owes as much to the fact that an account of a man's life is a coherent tale as it does to a general interest in other people—exceptional ones for preference, but often very ordinary ones will do. Even among professional historians, engaged in intellectually more demanding exercises within their chosen subject, those most widely read and longest remembered are tellers of tales. Who has not heard the praises of Frederic William Maitland sung? And who today, apart from some students and some working historians, reads him? Maitland wrote beautifully, far better than Trevelyan or Powicke or Arthur Schlesinger (Sr. or Jr.); among historians writing in English only Francis Parkman equals the direct appeal of his prose and only R. H. Tawney ever approached his ability to mix serious research with real wit. His themes may be heavy: the history of medieval law seems about as solemn a subject as a man may choose. Yet there is no more unpompous historian, none whom it is easier to enjoy. Everybody says so, including even those who have tried. Nevertheless, he never sold his books in the

* Notes for this chapter begin on p. 179.

numbers quite familiar to markedly lesser writers and was very properly published, unprofitably, by a highly respected University Press. No doubt, if he were alive today he would attract the attention of the many vigorous publishers who have discovered that one can sell quite real history to unexpectedly large circles of readers, but the point is that what he did write was all exceptionally readable and yet not widely read. He told no stories.

Of course, this preference for narrative has had its critics.[2] Dr. Leff, for instance, who will serve the case, throughout his *History and Social Theory*, fires off little broadsides at those (like the philosopher W. B. Gallie) who think that history is a story and its proper method is narrative. Ever since Lord Acton enjoined us, in one of the more overworked maxims to fall from even that august and bearded mouth, to study problems, not periods, historians who have wanted to be taken seriously by their fellows have been sure that their proper task lay in the analytical treatment of complex questions about the past. When, in the 1950's, the influence of Marc Bloch and the French *Annales* school—the first self-conscious school among real historians since the days of Ranke and Waitz a century before—extended beyond the original field of socioeconomic history to all forms of historical study, the great words became function and structure. This view of history rightly saw the events of the past all interlocking and interrelated, forming an indivisible unit which such conventional classifications as "social" or "political" or "intellectual" artificially destroyed. Wishing somehow to convey this overwhelming truth in the understanding of history (a truth which all reasonably competent historians grasp and assimilate, but none can put on paper), they held that the only way of writing history consists in taking a bit of the past to pieces before the reader's eyes and putting it together again, in the description of an organism or structure. In this way, all sorts of lines of approach and all sorts of not necessarily historical techniques can be deployed to the one end of re-creating a living reality in the past. The method is, in fact, strongly influenced by the social sciences; such structural and functional studies are really designed to produce historical sociology, which is not to say that they may not be good history as well. While this is unquestionably a perfectly proper thing to labor over, one may still question the conviction of enthusiasts and converts that it is the only way in which history should be written.

Quite apart from these high debates and fashions, the progress of historical research itself worked against narrative. As soon as the student comes to grips with the reality of the past, he becomes aware of two inescapable facts: the amount of evidential material which he needs to master, and the unsolved problems and questions which meet him at every turn. These facts of his existence combine to incline him to an analytical rather than a narrative method of working. Telling the tale becomes impossible when every few minutes one needs to stop in order to sort out an obscurity, and when one is continuously aware of reservations, complications, and refinements which render the brief summarizing sentences necessary in the flow of the story so crude and unsatisfactory to the aware scholar. Unquestionably, too, most serious historians will find greater intellectual satisfaction in the investigation and solution of analytical problems. They are then able to follow the problem wherever it leads, grasp it for themselves at first hand in all its aspects, and emerge with a task properly completed and a piece of proper understanding added to their own minds and to the general store of knowledge. By comparison, the satisfaction of telling a story (however complicated) is likely to be at best aesthetic, at worst meretricious. Analysis exercises above all the ratiocinative function, while narrative calls more upon the imagination:

and most practicing historians are rather longer on the first than on the second. Naturally so: if they were not they would no doubt write fiction, as some of the more imaginative occasionally do without admitting it (perhaps, one hopes, without knowing it).

I am thus very far from denying the cogency of the steadfast arguments against narrative and for analysis. Yet the structuralists, in whatever guise they may appear (and they include most economic historians as well as the whole powerful tribe of the social scientists among historians), call up one really overwhelming danger by their methods which can go all the way to wipe out the advantages of intellectual seriousness and penetration. They always hover on the edge of forgetting that history deals with events in time, that in history all things change and change continuously, though at varying rates. Anything that comes close to pretending a cross-section through a historical situation therefore perverts truth totally. Analysis and attention to structural function are forced to treat the historical material is that it be used to re-create life, to understand effectively as dead. The essential demand of all historical material is that it be used to recreate life, to understand and describe the life that produced these extant relics, and therefore to demonstrate the main manifestation of life, which is movement. The whole difficulty of historical reconstruction and writing lies in this fundamental truth about history: it contains a multiple situation forever on the move. Narrative tends to fall victim to the need to simplify the multiplicity and to disregard too many facets of the moving situation. But analysis, especially the more it succeeds in accommodating the multiple, has to help itself by ignoring the fact of motion. It may be only a matter of personal opinion which of these deficiencies one fears the more, but I should like to suggest that something a little more essential is involved. Without a very present sense of time and change, of life and death, history ceases altogether to be history, whereas a narrative devoid of the full range of past experience is still history, only not altogether adequate or satisfactory history. That is to say, the dangers inherent in analysis are fatal, those inherent in narrative only damaging.

It is perfectly true that neither danger needs to overwhelm the enterprise. Analytical history by no means needs to end by forgetting time and motion; the example of Maitland stands there to prove that this is so. Even when the lure of function, structure, and sociological enquiry augments the natural perils of the analytical method, the really good historian will still write good history, as Marc Bloch showed. But the signs unfortunately are that it takes an exceptional man to escape the dangers; and any reader in doubt is asked to undergo a prolonged course of reading in such journals (articles being shorter than books) as *Past and Present* or the *Economic History Review*, periodicals dedicated to the worship of structural analysis. I am not concerned with the undoubted stimulus of thought often provided by the first or the undoubted offences against the English language often committed by the second, but only with the question whether the meritorious and serious work published there still reflects or creates any instinctive sense of the past. Far too often the societies considered there (and elsewhere) could be anywhere and of any time— could be twentieth-century Tibet as readily as fifteenth-century England—because the method imposes an insufficient chronological discipline and induces no awareness of location in time. When the topic chosen and its temporal extent in particular are very restricted, the worst defects of the analytical method can be avoided, but this is done at the cost of forever writing pretty small-scale history. When the theme gets larger and the time span investigated longer, great care must be taken to remember the passage of time.

This gets harder as one retreats through the centuries because of the telescoping effect already mentioned.[3] Though "Colonial America" covers over 150 years, it is commonly spoken of as though it formed a single whole contrastable with postrevolutionary America, and much the same is true of all periods to which an effective descriptive name has been attached.

This, incidentally, is the chief peril involved in "periodization," the manner in which analysis pays its deceptive lip service to chronological reporting and a method for studying history which the problems of teaching have made so familiar to student and teacher alike. However carefully designed, periods are artificial devices, useful, of course, and legitimate as devices, but still quite unreal. When they are deliberately employed to make sense of history, and especially when they are treated as units (that is, analytically), they always end up by distorting truth because they insist on seeing the essence of the past in unities and common elements rather than in change and diversity.[4] The historian really needs to remain constantly aware and alert, especially in the presence of his own aids to understanding; whenever he handles problems, as inevitably he often will, he must at the back of his mind see the flow of time and the transformation which comes over the pieces of his problem even while he is analyzing it in structural and functional terms.

If I have rather labored the disasters attendant upon the analytical method, it is not because I wish to decry something that I have often practiced and shall often practice again, or perhaps because it alone traps its practitioners into major error. On the contrary, the method deserves all the praise it has received, nor is it at all more likely to manifest its characteristic faults than is narrative. But it happens at the present to be the professionals' preferred method, so that its difficulties are rarely stressed and its virtues are taken for granted; its superiority has achieved the status of an unexamined orthodoxy. The political historian must certainly be trained in employing it. Not only are the ancillary and subsidiary studies in political history —the treatment of constitutional or ideological questions, for instance—often bound to require analysis rather than narrative, but specifically political questions can call for it, too. Particular crises (as for instance the Munich crisis of 1938) can be well treated not by telling the story but by taking apart the circumstances and events which led to a particular main event; what really happened in a crisis and why can often be explained best (or only) without a given framework of the chronological flow. In such cases, as experience shows, narrative turns into a piece of journalistic reporting, unable to isolate and account for the real points of issue. Such obviously political problems as the relationship between a monarch and his advisers or the composition of a political party demand to be analyzed rather than told. Other forms of history more consistently ask the more obviously analytical questions, but that does not mean that the political historian asks none.

Nevertheless, the final product in the writing of political history cannot really be an analysis, a sorting out of structure, the study of a problem. In the last resort and the last outcome, there will be a story to tell and a sequence of events to be expounded. For the political historian, narrative is inescapable, and he must therefore reflect with some care upon its attendant problems. In the past, certainly, the propriety of storytelling had been taken too much for granted, with the result that when analytical history began to grow in strength, depth, and variety it had no difficulty in oversetting the balance and creating the present state of contemptuous hostility toward the oldest manner of all of writing history. Narrative came soon to be seen as inadequate because it was superficial: it took account of too few aspects of the past experience, it explained things too rationally and in fact rationalized the past beyond all probability, it overemphasized the function of individuals and ignored the conditions in which they labored, and in its devotion to the flow of time removed all landmarks that might have given not only memorability but even meaning to the confused welter of events. Charges of this sort have often enough been raised against political history as such when they should have been addressed to the political historian's preferred method of writing and not against the content of his subject matter. And often enough they have been true. Narrative, at one time universal and unquestioned, was rendered inefficient by two developments in the state of learning and knowledge. On the one hand, historical research itself has for a long time been engaged in enlarging the known area of the past, finding new topics, subtler problems, ramifying roads to understanding, all of which have at the very least been complicating the received picture of historical happenings beyond the point where, it seems, they can be incorporated into a proper narrative. For another, the progress of other studies concerned with man, as for instance psychology or anthropolgy, has increasingly cast doubt upon any manner of reporting the past in which events appear to be moved and to be carried by rational human beings pursuing identified ends in a purposeful way. Limited in its concerns, too superficial and ordered in its way of looking upon the past, narrative seems too often an inadequate method for making the past intelligible and no method at all for saying new things in history.

The question is whether this general condemnation can be upheld. Are the undoubted deficiencies unavoidable, and is the historian compelled to be either profound (for want of a better word) but always narrow and likely to be of interest only to other historians, or possibly interesting and lively enough to read but always at a level which can excite

no intellectual admiration and provide no intellectual satisfaction? I have before this adumbrated a first answer to
the question whether there is still room for the narrative
method in the serious and searching writing of history.[5] In
brief, I have suggested that a "modern" narrative, to satisfy
both the state of knowledge and the range of questions
rightly thought relevant in history today, needs to be built
around "lumps" of analysis. The main run of the writing
should follow the story, but the writer should take time off,
at irregular intervals and whenever it seems necessary, to
tackle a problem which requires analysis. The interruptions
of the story will vary in length, from a paragraph to perhaps a whole chapter (though preferably not the last).
There is nothing particularly original in this, though the
device is easier to prescribe than to practice and is not, in
actual fact, much practiced nowadays. The problems it
gives rise to are two: first, whether this change of pace and
manner is sufficient to rescue narrative from the charge of
superficiality, and second, whether it can be managed without breaking the flow and exasperating the reader. The first
is an intellectual problem, the second a stylistic one; but
both need to be solved if the method is to succeed in re-
creating adequate storytelling in history.

Traditionally, political narrative has usually included
passages of description or analysis. The famous third chapter of Macaulay's *History of England,* in which he laid
before the reader the social and political structure of the
community whose political life he was proposing to tell, was
such an insertion. Narrative historians of major events
commonly begin with some setting of the scene: Italy on
the eve of the Renaissance, Germany on the eve of the
Reformation or the Thirty Years' War, the American
colonies on the eve of Revolution, the United States on the
eve of the Civil War. This "on the eve" method is relatively
easy and offers an apparently effective opportunity for pro-

viding understanding in depth and range; in fact, it is unsatisfactory. The writer by this means succeeds in withdrawing from the narrative such matters as he will find difficult to accommodate in it: this is a legitimate advantage. He provides an understanding of the situation whose developments remain to be described: this in itself makes sense. However, the method conceals within it two serious faults. The relevance of the detail given in the scene-setting remains obscure to the reader, and there is a very serious danger that a form of contrived determinism enters inasmuch as the scene-setting chapter is almost bound to produce the effect of explaining all that follows.

The trouble with the first point is that a society "on the eve" of some development will contain elements which explain what happens next as well as a great many that do not; the historian runs the risk of either including the lot (and thereby detaching his chapter from the real purpose of the enterprise—destroying the ordered unity and explanatory capacity of his work), or of slanting the contents toward the outcome without admitting that that is what he is doing (thereby committing a form of confidence trick which destroys his capacity to persuade). As for the second fault, it involves the error of allowing situational causes to usurp the role which they are not fitted to play. If we were right in our analysis of causation, the events of the story must be directly explained by direct causes, but these last can form no part of the scene-setting chapter whose exclusive preoccupation is with situations and situational causes. In short, the "on the eve" method does not solve the problem of a fully explained and explanatory narrative because it detaches an essential part of the story-complex physically from the rest, treats it so differently as to make the break both manifest and stultifying, and instead of offering explanation at the point where it is wanted, begs the explanatory question before the reader knows what is to be explained. The same inadequacies can apply to chapters inserted later in the narrative, though the fact that he is in the middle of a story assists the historian and helps to protect him. As long as the analytical section analyzes a static situation conceived of in some way as relevant to the story of changing events, it is very likely both to fail to press home that relevance and to evade the duty of explanation by creating a sense of doom. In this way, too many readers, and also too many historians, become somehow convinced that a given historical development was inevitable, that it necessarily and inescapably derived and arose from the situation as described. This makes it easier to write ordered and meaningful and propagandist history, but it comes very close to being the historian's really cardinal sin.

Moreover, the scene-setting method has some difficulty even in fulfilling the task of creating real historical depth. It is, after all, description, not in itself a very penetrating method, and it always finds it hard to get from description to analysis (that is, to rational exposition and comprehension) because the details are necessarily paraded without reference to specific events or circumstances in the story to be told. We are back with the problems arising in historical explanation. Until one knows what is to be explained, anything may be said but nothing will convince, because only the fact to be explained renders meaningful the selection of situational causes offered by the historian. Chapters describing the scene before the event are in the nature of guidebooks, comprehensive or inadequate, but in no way systematic in relation to the journey to be undertaken. And in taking stock of his preliminary situation, the historian cannot achieve a deeper analysis because he cannot yet know what it is that really needs analyzing, or at any rate he cannot yet show what needs to be so treated. The "on the eve" method divorces situation from consequent event, begs explanatory problems, and fails to bring about the very thing it is supposed to do, the deepening of mere narrative. Any serious reader of history will be familiar with the double tedium created by so many of these chapters: the tedium of at least mild bewilderment at why these things are here described, and the tedium of having frequently to turn back to the introduction when suddenly a point in the narrative illumines the hitherto nonexistent relevance of an earlier passage. This occurs regularly, whether the historian is skillful or not, because it is a fault in the method, not in the practitioner. The "on the eve" method falls down on both counts: it provides neither that inclusion of analytical understanding nor that conclusive persuasion of the reader which need to be supplied if narrative is to regain its place.

The clue to the problem lies in a simple enough necessity: the historian wishing to write narrative must take narrative seriously. He must mean it. That is to say, he must in the first place want to write a piece which is narrative throughout, in which narrative not only forms a main skeleton but dominates every part of the structure. It may be worth pointing out that this does not imply the writing of absolutely continuous narratives; if the story to be told is complex and large enough, it may well be necessary and desirable to write a kind of interwoven narrative in which different chapters take up different topics with different chronological divisions, all running side by side and knitting together, but all essentially narrative. If the historian sets his mind thus, he will not be tempted to cast any specially selected section of the work in the analytical or descriptive form but will resort to this alternative method only when something in the narrative definitely calls for it. This can and does happen at any point in the story. The difficulty is to remain alert and receptive to the call, to know all the time that this or that needs going into; the only prescription, for what it is worth, is to tell the historian never to say anything that he has not explained, or least made plain, to himself, and then to allow the reader to become as well instructed as himself. As he tells the story of a political quarrel, the institutions and instruments and personalities used in the quarrel must be fully understood if the story is to be fully understood. As he tells the story of a war, he cannot really make it plain unless he has achieved a thorough grasp of the means and purposes of the combatants: it will be necessary to discuss the art of war, the distribution of armed strength, the machinery of diplomacy, the social and economic facts behind a national or dynastic policy, and so forth. In practice, we all do something of this when we write any sort of history: no one, not even perhaps the simplest of chroniclers, has ever confined his narrative to just that, a stringing together of events with never an analytical sentence in it. All that is here proposed is that the political historian should consciously enlarge a natural and obvious method by enlarging his analytical insertions into real analysis, a real and exhaustive dissection of the problems which the particular stage of his narrative throws up.

Ideally, this should be done without stopping or starting, without the signaling of a break, and without any resumptive commonplaces of the "thus we see" variety. If the analysis required is brief, no problem arises. If it is prolonged, art may nevertheless succeed in making it grow naturally out of a piece of storytelling and again merge painlessly into the continuation of the story at the far end. There is no point in pursuing these notions any further here; in these matters (which are certainly important to the end product), everything depends on the powers of literary skill and imaginative integration brought to the task by the historian. All that I can do, or wish to do, is to stress the real need to remember such problems of the craft, to remember that writing itself is a challenge to the historian quite as severe and quite as vital as the challenge of the question to be answered, the problem to be resolved, the history to be understood. The end in view is a story so told as to explain itself in full, not because (as some philosophers suppose) storytelling in itself is equal to explanation,[6] but because the narrative (which itself answers "how" questions) has included within it, at the right places, the analytical answering of "why" questions and the descriptive answering of "what" questions; it is a story, moreover, so told in this fashion that no reader could fail to note that he is being told a story, not being presented with a succession of sections or chapters.[7]

Let us, then, assume that the writing of this kind of narrative is possible because it is really necessary: that narrative can be "thickened" by passages of analysis naturally arising out of the issues brought to the fore by the narrative itself. Let us also agree, if only for the sake of the argument, that the common device of scene-setting and explanatory chapters fails of its purpose, for the reasons already stated. That still leaves us with a difficult question. The method here proposed may well result in a reasonably intelligent and intelligible narrative, producing explanation and understanding in a, so to speak, organic fashion, and persuading the mind by attaching analytical discussion to particular points of the historical process described. It may carry the reader from story to explanation and back to story without serious disturbance; more important, perhaps, it may force the historian himself to move from one to the other as need dictates, thus preventing him from leaving things unexplained, pointlessly intruded, or explained by the circular arguments of determinism. But how thorough can this method be? How complete can it render the situation within which the historical narrative occurs? How fully can it explore the points of analysis required? How original and searching can it be in the asking of questions? Have we, in fact, succeeded in removing the charge of superficiality? Quite specifically, remembering what were stated to be the two chief reasons for the opprobrium in which narrative finds itself, is it possible in this way to take account of the discoveries which have broadened historical knowledge so extensively outside the old political field, and of the discoveries which have broadened and transformed our knowledge of the inner and outer influences upon human action?

Between them, these massive additions to the historian's knowledge and to his armory have certainly rendered many traditional stories out-of-date, or (properly speaking) not so much inadequate as plainly wrong. But from the political historian's point of view, the effects of these various advances are not all the same. No obviously intractable problem attaches to the need to incorporate additional bits of knowledge about the past where these move in the same aura as the knowledge already there; and a great deal of historical and other research produces just such new traditional history, making the picture and the story more precise and fuller without forcing a transformation in it. To write political history today, one must certainly acquaint oneself with all that is being learned about the lives of the societies whose history is being written. All the questions and answers which structural analysis handles concerning population, economy, the social realities of power, and all the other sophisticated details which are receiving attention must become familiar to the political historian. In the first place, he will, of course, have to learn a good deal: that is, he will have to accept specific arguments and conclusions at second hand. This is not a serious matter, for no historian has ever written who did not in some measure rely on the work of others. Though he should do some checking, both perhaps by reworking this or that problem and more certainly by applying critical tests of sense, probability, and coherence to the findings of others, he not only need not refuse their help but should be most active in seeking it.

Where the outcome of these parallel labors consists of specific solutions to particular problems—for instance, a theory of kingship, a demonstrable shift in the social structure, the clarification of the law on a given point—the political historian will have no difficulty in absorbing the new matter into his story, either by rewriting the story itself or by including a summary of the analytical work in the manner already suggested. This sort of thing happens all the time, and the difference between real narrative history and the common-run textbook is marked by the degree to which the writer has "kept up," has really assimilated the progress of the study. Those historians of politics who practice analytical study in their own territory (as it might be, in some problem of government) will best be able to treat the findings of others as they would treat their own. It might be asserted as a pedagogic fact that no one should attempt to write narrative who has not provided extensive proof of analytical ability.

The difficulties are of quite a different order when the progress of historical research has led not simply to new knowledge of the old kind but has produced a serious shift in attitudes to society past and present. Here the work of historical analysis links hands with the new insights derived from the kinds of social science which, as I have suggested, introduce the other grave doubt about traditional narrative in modern historical writing. By the time that structural analysis, itself stimulated by the example of sociology, has done its work, and by the time that historians have really absorbed the teachings of social psychology and social anthropology, the historian may well be faced not with a traditional story that needs correcting and enlarging, but with a situation in which the whole traditional historical interpretation is called into question. This is certainly what most social scientists and a good many historians would like to think will happen. For instance, a history of the French Revolution built round constitutional reform, personal ambitions, and conflicts, the problems of international interference, the events of the Terror and the rise of Napoleon, can be amended and thoroughly altered in many details while still remaining essentially the same story. It is possible to replace the mob of the faubourgs by Professor Rudé's respectable artisans, or to remember the provinces in a story traditionally centered on Paris, without having to face any real abolition of major parts of the narrative. But if one wants to take account of the kind of analysis provided by Soboul, or alternatively wishes to allow for the light thrown on human behavior by the investigations of the last sixty years, one is increasingly driven to abandon both the story and the storytelling method in favor of a treatment which becomes mainly analytical and stresses elements quite different from those highlighted in the narrative accounts. Is there any point in taking the reader through the events of the Directory when what matters is the clash of groups or even of impersonal forces? What is one to do with the details of constitutions and concordats when what was really going on depended on problems of industrialization and resistance to it? Every major or minor historical narrative can come up against questions of this sort as soon as the often perfectly correct insights of analysis, rather than its particular conclusions, are to be taken into the story. After E. P. Thompson's *The Making of the English Working Class*,[8] can anyone write a history of the Industrial Revolution in England which turns on such things as technological advance or the accumulation and use of capital? The answer is, I very much hope so; but one sees the difficulties.

No general answer can be given to these questions, especially the question of how justified the historian can be who continues to treat history as the product of human action. It should be remembered that when all is done even

the new history, with its graphs, analyses, and recognition
of the impersonal and irrational elements in past events,
still of necessity thinks in terms of people: otherwise it
would not be history at all. No matter how much more
complex and impenetrable the past becomes as knowledge
accumulates, it still remains a story of human existence
and activity. It is certainly possible to absorb a great deal
of all the new matter into political narrative, even where it
goes beyond the addition to knowledge of the traditional
type into a genuine transformation of beliefs about human
society. This is not, after all, the first time that historians
have faced precisely this sort of situation. The work of the
great Renaissance historians like Guicciardini, of Mon-
tesquieu and Vico, of the discoverers of the documentary
record from the Bollandists onward, or of the scientific
historians of the nineteenth century, invariably produced
and assimilated not only more knowledge but knowledge of
the transforming kind. Nor is the present situation so much
more overwhelming than those precedents were. Far more
and more intensive work is going forward, but for one
thing, the aids to keeping up with it (bibliographies,
summaries, technical help like films) are also improving,
and for another, mass does not here equal quality.

This brings us to a delicate and difficult point. So far
I have accepted the claims of the new discoveries and their
alleged effect upon the value of narrative at their own esti-
mation. Those who decry narrative and believe only in the
analytical method do so because the complexity of the past
cannot for them be expounded or explained in a story, and
because they are anxious to achieve the sort of scientific
penetration into past societies which they believe the modern sciences can accomplish for contemporary societies.
These are laudable ambitions, but they are also somewhat
exaggerated. The social sciences have not really been notably successful so far in giving a more profound under-

standing of man's contemporary situation, unless one accepts without question many artificial statements of the obvious or manifest misstatements disproved by experience; by and large, historians have been at least as informative about the past as their brethren have been about the present. Both groups of scholars are trying out the virtue of new tools, exemplified in such fashionable enterprises as those concerned with family restitution, or social mobility, or decision-making, or normative convictions. The historian (the traditional historian) can contribute as much to them as he can derive from others: the past, as has been said often enough before, is the social scientist's laboratory, and the historian is the person who equips the laboratory and defines the experiments. He will do well to preserve some skepticism toward the theories and semiempirical discoveries which are pressed upon him from every side. We are constantly assured, especially by those still learning to practice intellectual disciplines at all, that there can be no history without theory, that the historian who has no guiding interpretative theories writes no history worth the naming. But we may fairly reply that the historian who writes his history to a theory, who sees the past in the light of analytical methods developed without a proper study of the past's extant record, neglects the first condition of his proper calling and writes no history at all. A theory is only as good as its proofs, and the striking thing about most social theories that I have ever encountered—especially when they try to bring into focus large and complex situations—is their failure to answer to the facts; they always end by ignoring the inconvenient.[9]

The historian should indeed learn all he can about humanity and its social existence; these are the themes of his enquiry. He needs, therefore, to rethink his history in the light of what he and others can add to understanding on all these themes, and he will assuredly find himself enlarg-

ing the area of study and refining the explanatory interpretations all the time. But it is also his particular place
in the common enterprise to act as a critic and a control.
Time and again, the findings of social analysis run counter
to the experience of the past, and one of the more impres-
sive things about the social sciences today is the way in
which they are going into history, are acquiring a historical dimension. Too often they meet historians who are over-
awed by them, so that the corrective is not applied. If it
is true, as it is, that the historian who would write today as
he would have written fifty years ago deserves only oblivion,
it is equally true that the man who accepts the latest constructs of the theorists and analysts without subjecting
them to the skeptical treatment to which historians are
trained in their own trade will write history that tomorrow
will be forgotten. And the test which in the end he has to
apply is narrative.

History is the study of mankind's fortunes through the
ages, and if it cannot be told as a story it can no longer be
history. No one, to say it once more, wishes to write down
analysis; the study of problems, the dissection of situations,
these are essential parts of every historian's task. Yet he has
not fully achieved his purpose unless he has also assimilated his knowledge of the past into a tale, a piece of narrative progressing through time. The ability to write historical narrative is not only the historian's personal test; it is
also the test of the sort of history on which he is working.
The story may be short or long, simple or complex, but the
element of story has to be there if what he is producing is
to be history. There is, therefore, really no point in the
attack on narrative by historians who appreciate the fact
that for the purposes of achieving understanding most fully
and most deeply narrative is as a rule useless. The analytical labors and their results are, in the last resort, only
stages toward the sort of understanding which produces a

narrative. Our problem today is not whether to write narrative or not, but what sort of narrative we should write.
And even here we are less free to choose than we might
like. The tyranny of time (and of dates) together with the
limitations set to knowledge by the surviving evidence
create a main structure of stories which cannot be readily
altered or avoided.

As I have tried to show throughout this book, that structure will be overwhelmingly political, overwhelmingly concerned with those fortunes and manipulations of power in
society which form the main recorded activities of men and
embody, even if they do not cause, the facts of change,
variety, and transformation which differentiate the static
picture of theory from the moving picture of fact. Of course,
a political narrative should not forget the nonpolitical concerns of man, all of which, in one way or another, contribute to his existence in society and therefore to the story of
social action, the story of politics. All the forms of history
that have existed, exist now, or may yet come to exist belong to the world which the political historian inhabits. If
at times he may feel, perhaps too arrogantly, that they exist
only in order to amplify, explain, and put right his political
story, he needs to be humbler and recall that politics are
not for most people the content of daily life; yet all things
are relevant to politics. The political historian therefore
must certainly know the duty of understanding what his
colleagues are doing and saying; he must absorb their answers to their problems if his answers to his are to have
virtue and validity.

How he is to achieve this synthesis of the ever more
complex mass of facts, structures, and understandings remains his problem, but that he must attempt it seems clear
to me, as it also seems clear that he must achieve his end
without the Greek gift of an ordering theory that offers
answers in despite of the evidence. After decades of ever

more intensive work on details and very particular problems—work that quite rightly still goes on all the time, for there is still very much to do—and decades of rethinking the known facts of the past in the light of theory and insight, historians now need consciously to return to their first duty. Let them once again tell stories, real stories, though far from simple stories. The task is, indeed, very difficult. The mass of books pouring forth at this moment includes many that allegedly deal with this or that period of history; books, that is, which do not pretend to concern themselves with a particular analytical question but with a piece of multiple human history. Yet far too many of these books escape the dilemmas by falling back on analysis, on chapters which deal in turn with this or that "aspect" of the chosen period's life. Only those who have never tried to write narrative would mock these efforts: one well understands how impossibly gigantic the task of bringing all that knowledge and interpretation into the framework of a story must have seemed. Nevertheless, we may be at the point where it were better to write a flawed narrative than a successful collection of analytical chapters.

The new narratives will be thick with the results as well as the exposition of analysis. They will be more chary of ascribing things to personal action and surface motive. They will remember the society behind the individuals, unsolved problems among those that have been solved, the conditions that govern man as well as the choices that enable men to dominate conditions. They will extend the concerns of politics beyond the public action of the leading figures and bring out the ramification of power through society, through mankind. They will be written by historians who have gained a better understanding of structure, minds, and motives without having abandoned their own professional responsibility to evidence, reason, and critical assessment. They will (one hopes) manage to be exciting without being superficial, swift without losing depth. In particular they will, I trust, remember that not all history is solemn, serious, heavy, and dull: the human comedy is not all tragic.

I do not pretend, even to myself, that what I have been able to say about the problems of narrative history really solves the difficulties which the historian encounters in practice. Those he must solve as he comes to them and as best he can; and if he really means to tell the present world about its past he will so solve them. For he cannot then rest content until, fully experienced in the handling of historical enquiry in all its forms, he has put together a story which is a history.

Enough of these reflections. It is high time to return to the thing itself.

NOTES

1. Biography of the, let us say, lively sort is very popular in England, perhaps less so in the United States where a high and serious vein produces those massive multivolume "lives" of statesmen thoughtful enough to have left behind large and well-ordered archives.

2. For a philosophic discussion of narrative and its problems, see the argument between Maurice Mandelbaum, Richard G. Ely, Rolf Gruner, and William H. Dray in *History and Theory* 6 (1967): 413–419, and 8 (1969): 275–294. I am once again troubled by the inescapable signs that people are here talking about something they have never attempted to do.

3. Above, p. 66.

4. This is one trouble with Dr. Leff's preference for periodization over other forms of meaningful construction in the understanding of the past (*History and Social Theory* [London, 1969], ch. 7): it does not give to analysis the dimension of temporal passage, but rather ossifies the passage of time in large unitary chunks. The other trouble is that no periods ever apply to more than one section of mankind and usually only to part of that section's experience. Witness the difficulties encountered by the attempts to fix a divide

between "the middle ages" and "modern times." The answers offered by those who look to religion, politics, or exploration differ from the answers of those who study ideas or social habits; and historians of art, of science, or technology beg to differ again. Yet they all apply themselves to the same part of the world (Europe), and in their own terms they are all justified.

5. *Practice of History* (London and New York, 1967), p. 131ff.

6. It sometimes is and sometimes is not. In identifying narrative as the historian's method of explanation, W. B. Gallie (*Philosophy and Historical Understanding* [London, 1964]) perhaps had in mind the sort of analysis-thickened narrative I recommend, in which case the argument is sound but requires analyzing further because the alleged explanatory method itself involves varieties of explanation.

7. I pointed out in *Practice of History*, p. 138f., that I tried, with limited success, to write such narrative in my *Reformation Europe* (1963). I refer to that passage for more detail, but I may add that I remain ambitious to do more of this sort of thing, and do it better.

8. New York, 1964.

9. Cf. *Practice of History*, ch. 1. An interesting study could be made of E. J. Hobsbawm, an excellent historian whose history is guided by theory (i.e., Marxism). He has written both on the nineteenth century, where he is truly expert, and on the seventeenth which he does not know well at first hand. The former work will stand; the latter is quite another matter.

INDEX

Acton, John Dahlberg Lord, 158
Aehrenthal, Aloys von, 14
Analytical method, 159–163, 172–174
Aristotle, 3, 44, 46
Athens, 60, 63

Bainville, Jacques, 116
Barraclough, Geoffrey, 120–121, 136
Bede, 75, 82
Bentham, Jeremy, 86
Bismarck, Otto von, 14, 20, 100
Bloch, Marc, 158, 161
Bolingbroke, Oliver St. John Viscount, 46
Bollandists, 174
Books as historical material, 105–107
Bowker, Margaret, 109 (n. 10)
Bracton, Henry de, 44
Britain, Battle of, 98
Burton, J. W., 54 (n. 6)
Busch, Briton C., 54 (n. 2)
Butler, James R. M., 21
Butterfield, Herbert, 109 (n. 23)

Caesar, Julius, 45, 75, 114
Calder, Isabel M., 109 (n. 4)
Cantor, Norman F., 153 (n. 16)
Castlereagh, Robert Steward Lord, 13–14
Causes in History: classified, 138; covering-law theories, 125–126; defined, 136–137, 141–142, 150, 154 (n. 33); direct, 138–140, 143–144; imprecision theories, 132–135; not always discoverable, 135–136; situational,

138–140, 144–145; *see also* Conjecture, Laws, Proof
Charlemagne, 76
Charles I (king of England), 107
Charles V (emperor), 138, 141, 143, 155 (n. 35)
Chronology, 65–67
Churchill, Winston S., 70–71
Cicero, 47–48, 109 (n. 18)
Clarendon, Edward Hyde, earl of, 76
Clarendon, George Villiers, earl of, 14
Clark, G. Kitson, 55 (n. 10)
Clarke, Aidan, 109 (n. 21)
Cleon, 46
Cobban, A. B., 54 (n. 3)
Collingwood, R. G., 122, 133
Communist Manifesto, 115
Conjecture, legitimate, 145–149
Cooper, John P., 55 (n. 12)
Croce, Benedetto, 116, 122, 129–130, 133, 154 (n. 26)
Cromwell, Oliver, 93
Cromwell, Thomas, 46, 55 (n. 28), 87, 93, 109 (n. 12), 138, 147–149
Crowe, Eyre, 13

Danto, Arthur D., 124, 150, 152 (n. 1), 155 (n. 41)
Darwin, Charles, 14
Domesday Book, 87
Donagan, Alan, 114–115, 125, 152 (n. 1), 153 (n. 18)
Doucet, R., 32
Dray, William, 114, 117, 124, 132–135, 152 (n. 1), 154 (nn. 23, 27, 33), 179 (n. 2)